Courage to Cure Codependency

Healthy Detachment Strategies to Overcome Jealousy in Relationships, Stop Controlling Others, Boost Your Self Esteem, and Be Codependent No More

LEAH CLARKE

CONTENTS

"Many of us live in denial of who we truly are because we fear losing someone or something and there are times that if we don't rock the boat, too often the one we lose is ourselves...It feels good to be accepted, loved, and approved of by others, but often the membership fee to belong to that club is far too high of a price to pay."

Dennis Merritt Jones

INTRODUCTION

You may not realize this right now, but getting this book is an extremely meaningful part of your journey to prevent codependency, heal from codependency, or cure your codependency and engage in healthier relationships in your life. I know from personal experience that moving away from codependency and into healthier behavioral patterns is not easy and can often be quite painful, so your willingness to invest in yourself and your commitment to experience healthier interactions in your life prove just how strong and how ready you are to begin your new life without codependency.

Throughout this book, we will be exploring principles and healing techniques of codependency with the support of information from licensed therapists, counselors, psychologists, doctors, and psychological studies from around the world. As you work through this book, you are going to discover what a healthy relationship truly looks like and why your current relationship may not reflect one that is healthy and fulfilling. You will understand that being in a healthy relationship requires both individuals taking responsibility for themselves and their capacity to have their needs met while having compassion and empathy towards each other and their partner's needs.

This is not only the case in romantic relationships, either. The same dynamic applies to any healthy relationship, whether it is one that you share with a romantic partner, a family member, a friend, or even a coworker. Adhering to these healthy boundaries and approaching your current or future relationship with the desire to enrich each other's lives without becoming caretakers for each other is extremely important. This ensures that you are both able to function as fully independent people, while enjoying the healthy, fulfilling company of each other during your shared interactions.

If you have never been in a healthy relationship before, you may not have a strong understanding of what it is that you are trying to work toward. To you, a mutually beneficial relationship of two people coming together as independent individuals to share a relationship that is not all-consuming may be foreign. In fact, it might even sound somewhat uncomfortable to you.

Engaging in an unhealthy, all-consuming relationship may even be something that you're doing that you don't even realize. Or it may be the direction that you're headed in if you're not careful and remain on the same seemingly mildly dysfunctional path you are on now. Right now, you may even be holding on to a vision of an ideal relationship that is tainted by codependent perceptions, thus, your current desires may include some degree of toxicity.

Right now, you may be experiencing a relationship that is rich in the common symptoms of codependency. You could be completely aware of the dysfunction in your relationship, or in the previous relationships you have been in, yet you do not necessarily know how to fix it. Maybe you do not even realize that the dysfunction results from codependency at this point.

To you, the idea of being in a relationship where you take care of everything and everyone and continually take the blame for others' consequences may seem normal. It may not seem unreasonable that you put your needs aside in order to give the other person exactly what they want while you go without yet again. In fact, you may even fail to realize that you are being taken advantage of, or that there is a way for you to stop being taken advantage of by the other person. At this point, you may have no idea that these very behaviors are what contribute to the dysfunction being experienced in your relationships.

Regardless of whether you are someone who has already discovered that you are codependent or if you are not yet aware of your codependent behaviors, this book is a powerful resource to support you in overcoming codependency. You will attain the resolve you need whether you are in a relationship you want to improve, looking to heal from a previous codependent relationship, or aiming to avoid getting into a codependent relationship. Knowing how to properly approach codependency and heal it effectively will ensure that you have the capacity to stop letting others take you for granted and to start engaging in healthy relationships that involve both give *and* take.

The best way to ensure that you get the most out of this book is to begin by reading part one and understanding exactly what codependency is, the seemingly innocuous manifestations of it, and the ways you may be exhibiting it without realizing it. You may find that everything does not apply to you, and you may discover things you never thought about or realized that do apply to you.

Pay extra close attention to what the experts have to say and what various studies have shown in terms of how codependency impacts individuals and why, so that you can gain a greater sense of self-awareness around the issue. Then, move on to part two where you can begin exploring tactics you can implement to begin healing from codependency, no matter what stage of a relationship you are in, and even if you are not currently in a relationship.

Part two is laid out in three easy chapters, each of which will walk you through seven steps you need to complete in order to heal from codependency depending on where you are at in your life. If you are avoiding codependency in future relationships, currently in a codependent relationship, or healing from the ending of a codependent relationship, you will find exactly what you need to support you in overcoming negative patterns and engaging in healthy behaviors.

Through reading these chapters, you are going to gain access to what numerous experts consider to be the necessary steps for any codependent to overcome their codependency. You do not have to continue being walked all over and trapped in unhealthy relationships that suck the life out of you, while giving you barely anything in return. You also do not have to live a life where you feel a constant sense of lack or a desperate need for approval and validation from those outside of you. Your relationship with yourself can become the most valuable one that you have, and you can learn how to give yourself the things you need so that you can live your best life and engage in the best relationships possible with the people around you.

Your best is yet to come and it starts here and now with you embracing your *Courage to Cure Codependency*.

LEAH CLARKE

Part 1:
Defining Codependency

CHAPTER 1:
WHAT IS
CODEPENDENCY?

According to the *Oxford Dictionary*, codependency is defined as an "excessive emotional or psychological reliance on a partner—typically, a partner who requires support due to an illness or addiction." However, our understanding on what codependency is has broadened significantly over the years, allowing us to have a greater understanding of what codependency truly is and how it affects people.

Individuals who are codependent have a tendency to portray extreme dependence upon others in their lives. According to the opinion of various psychologists and researchers, this dependence can be social, emotional, and sometimes, even physical.

These dependencies are believed to be the way in which codependent individuals are able to feel as though their needs are being fulfilled, though this belief is often an illusion. Essentially, these individuals are unclear as to how they can healthily meet their needs, so they use codependency as a coping method to attempt to satisfy themselves and feel fulfilled.

A study done by *Knudson & Terrell* in 2012 declared that codependency creates a major dysfunction in individuals, as it leads to codependent individuals forgetting to take care of themselves in favor of taking care of others. In addition to excessively taking care of others, a codependent person may also take unnecessary responsibility for others, such as blaming themselves for someone else's behavior.

The combination of these two extreme tendencies can lead to a disturbance in the development of their individual identity. As a result, many codependent individuals actually struggle to discern their own needs and interests apart from the individual that they experience their codependency towards.

The unique defining characteristic of codependency is that people who are codependent find themselves depending upon only one person. In other similar disorders with an element of dependency, that dependency is often distributed onto many other individuals. The amount of dependency placed upon a single individual in codependency is incredibly high, often reaching unhealthy levels that do not benefit the codependent individual nor the person whom they have become dependent on.

Codependency and Other Psychological Considerations

Currently, codependency is not recognized as a distinct personality disorder. However, it does share many overlapping similarities between several personality disorders that are distinctly recognized and diagnosable. Despite not being a diagnosable condition, many psychologists and researchers continue to use the term as a way to describe the possession of a specific set of characteristics that many individuals seem to portray.

In 1986, Dr. Timmen L. Cermak published a book on the topic entitled *Diagnosing and Treating Codependence*. In his book, he proposed that codependency ought to be a diagnosable personality disorder, worthy of being included in the *Diagnostic and Statistical Manual*, or *DSM*, which is used to diagnose and treat individuals with disorders. He discussed how codependency can be distinguished separately from other previously-recognized conditions and that, by officially recognizing codependency as its own condition, treatments could become more readily available. Unfortunately, his motion was denied, as the subsequent edition of the *DSM* did not include codependency as its own diagnosis.

One major reason why Dr. Cermak pushed towards having codependency recognized as an actual distinctive personality disorder is because it shares many common traits with other personality disorders that are commonly diagnosed. Still, it does not completely fit the description of any of the other disorders that are commonly mentioned.

Some of the conditions that codependency overlaps with include alcohol dependence, borderline personality disorder (BPD), dependent personality disorder (DPD), histrionic personality disorder, and post-traumatic stress disorder (PTSD). It is believed that the idea of identifying codependency as its own disorder has been dismissed because of how much it overlaps with DPD and BPD. Despite these overlaps, however, a study was done by psychologist Eva Knapek in 2017 that discovered that codependency can be exhibited without exhibiting symptoms of DPD or BPD. As such, despite its initial absence in the *DSM*, codependency is now commonly recognized as its own disorder that requires a unique approach when it comes to treating those who portray its symptoms.

The key area in which Knapek was able to distinguish codependency as a separate disorder was primarily in the fact that it does not include a dependency on a wide variety of people. This creates instability in interpersonal relationships by preventing the individual from willingly developing and nurturing relationships with others, while excessively nurturing their relationship with the one person they are dependent on.

The History of the Term "Codependency"

Codependency was first recognized in the Alcoholics Anonymous program in 1950, where individuals were able to begin understanding that in many cases, the symptoms of alcoholism were not entirely the addict's problem. The original term for codependency was "co-alcoholic" which was used to recognize the involvement of an individual's loved ones and how it affected their addictions. It was recognized that in many cases, alcoholics moved towards addiction as a way to cope with dysfunctional families and friends who had contributed to the individual's life.

In this circumstance, Alcoholics Anonymous used codependency as a way to explain how the loved ones of the alcoholic may interfere with their ability to heal from the addiction by over-helping the individual. In other words, their family or friends would excessively take care of them and take responsibility for their behaviors, thus preventing the addict from taking responsibility for themselves and their own needs.

The *Merriam-Webster Dictionary* still recognizes codependency in a way that distinctly acknowledges this history of the condition. Their definition is "a psychological condition or a relationship in which a person is controlled or manipulated by another who is affected with a pathological condition (such as an addiction to alcohol or heroin.)"

Through this definition, you can clearly understand how codependency can negatively impact both people in circumstances that involve addiction. While the codependency is often blamed on the codependent individual who over-helps the addict, it is actually believed to be a manipulative circumstance where the addict grooms the codependent to behave that way. This is an opportunity for the addict to avoid taking responsibility for their actions and their addictive behaviors so that they can continue abusing substances while placing the blame elsewhere.

Over time, psychologists realized that codependent behaviors could be seen elsewhere, too. In most of these circumstances, the individual who became the codependent grew to be that way as a result of dysfunctional home life or being conditioned by an individual with a mental health disorder. As a result, codependency is often believed to be a psychological response to living in unhealthy circumstances where the individual who becomes codependent is repeatedly manipulated until they reach that state.

The "Codependency Movement"

After the concept of codependency was introduced by Alcoholics Anonymous, psychologists started looking into the term and recognizing that it existed outside of relationships that involved addicted individuals. This is when the "codependency movement" was introduced. It is believed that the roots of the codependency movement lie in the theories produced by Karen Horney, a German psychoanalyst.

In 1941, Horney proposed that codependency was a personality style that people moved toward as a way to overcome their basic anxiety. As they repeatedly experience one or more needs going unmet, they begin to use codependency as a way to control those around them so as to fulfill their needs.

For example, in a narcissistic relationship, a narcissist conditions their victim by repeatedly giving and withholding love and affection from their partner. They also repeatedly shame and blame their partners, leaving their partner feeling not only as though their needs are unmet, but that their unmet needs are their own fault.

As a result, individuals foster codependent behaviors as a way to control having their needs met. They begin attempting to control the narcissist by acting in a codependent manner so that they can feel as though they are experiencing love, affection, and approval. Of course, the relationship between a narcissist and their victim goes much deeper than this, but this example can give you an idea of how the dynamic grows in relationships that are void of addiction.

Codependents can become codependent for a variety of reasons, but the primary driving force is their desire to have their needs met. Their dependency is essentially a subconscious opportunity for them to attempt to control the other individual through a dependent approach. Through placing an intense dependency upon one person, they pressure that individual into fulfilling their needs and helping them to feel psychologically and emotionally complete.

As a result of Karen Horney's proposal, psychologists began to identify how codependency could fit into many different relationships. They also began to understand why many people displayed codependent behaviors despite not being a part of relationships where addiction was present. As such, this became known as the "codependent movement," as codependency became more widely known and treated by therapists all over the world.

Who Codependency Affects

Codependency is not known to affect any person who identifies with a specific gender, ethnicity, culture, religion, or other individually defining demographic. Instead, codependency truly can impact anyone. In a general sense, codependency is most likely to impact anyone who undergoes a prolonged period of feeling as though their needs are unmet.

Individuals who are considered at risk of developing codependency include anyone who is involved in a close relationship with someone who has a chemical dependency or who is chronically mentally ill. However, there are many forms of familial dysfunction that can lead to an individual becoming codependent.

If you are an individual who shows signs of codependency, chances are that the person that you exhibit these signs towards is someone who is close to you in your network of friends and family. This could be your parent, sibling, spouse, best friend or even a co-worker.

The Causes of Codependency

As we have already identified previously in this chapter, codependency is primarily caused by dysfunctional families. The belief is that these individuals are most likely to develop a codependent tendency because they grow up believing that they don't matter or that their family problems are their fault.

A study was done in 2014 in Brazil by Bortolon, Barros, and Ferigolo at the Federal University of Health Sciences of Porto Alegre. This study looked into the family functions of individuals with codependency. Through studying 505 family members who were involved in close relationships with individuals who suffered from addiction, they discovered who was most likely to experience codependency and what those families looked like. The key takeaway was that the individuals who were most likely to become codependent were mothers or wives of addicts, who were unemployed and had less than 8 years of education.

What the study discovered was that individuals who were codependent likely became that way because taking care of someone else was their "primary job." When someone did not have a job or any other significant involvements or obligations in their lives, they were able to become heavily consumed by the process of taking care of someone else. Slowly, these individuals become all-consumed by the caretaking process to the point that they no longer seem to distinguish themselves as separate entities that are complete on their own.

While this caretaking factor was the key contributor to individuals developing codependent behaviors, there were two other things that became recognized as the likely causes of codependency. The first factor that made people more likely to become codependent was if they were raised in a house where a codependent dynamic existed between their parents. Because this individual was not shown a healthy relationship shared by their parents, they were less likely to understand how to engage in a healthy relationship of their own when they reached adulthood.

The second contributing factor was in households where the child became the codependent to a parent at a young age—for example, if one of their parents was a narcissist or an addict. In these unfortunate relationships, children are often groomed to take the blame for the family's dysfunction while also experiencing a lack of affection, acceptance, or recognition by their parent. Since children are highly impressionable, being exposed to codependent behaviors in their formative years can result in them struggling to identify the difference between a healthy and unhealthy relationship later in life.

As such, they often find themselves displaying the same behaviors that they watched or were conditioned to portray in childhood. This often results in the individual finding themselves in dysfunctional relationships where the other person either struggles with addiction or chronic mental health. This is likely because this is where the codependent feels most comfortable and can successfully implement their codependent behaviors.

CHAPTER 2:
ARE YOU
CODEPENDENT?

Codependent people often struggle to identify themselves as codependent because they believe that they are simply taking care of others. Because their codependent behaviors are rooted in their subconscious mind, they genuinely believe that they are doing the right thing and that there is no other alternative. As a result, it can be a challenge to recognize if you are a codependent individual or not.

Understanding if you truly are just a caring person or if you are struggling with codependency is important. While being caring and compassionate is a generally positive trait, being codependent can be extremely destructive. As a codependent, the need to take care of others extends beyond compassion for others by hitting a little closer to home. Rather than being a genuinely selfless act, codependency is the process of taking care to the extreme, often overlooking your own needs in favor of someone else's. As a result, it can lead to severe psychological, emotional, and sometimes, even physical consequences.

If you identify as an individual who was raised around or who currently lives around individuals who struggle with addiction or chronic mental health, it is imperative that you take the time to pay close attention to this chapter. Identifying your own personality traits and discovering if they align with that of a codependent individual can support you in understanding yourself to a deeper degree. Through this understanding, you can seek to effectively treat your codependent tendencies so that you can have your needs met in a way that is not destructive to yourself or to anyone else.

Signs of a Codependent Personality

Although codependency is not seen as its own distinctive personality disorder, there are many specific signs that can determine whether or not someone is experiencing codependency in their life. It is important that if you begin considering yourself or someone else as being codependent, you should clearly understand what the true signs and symptoms are.

Unfortunately, many people loosely throw around the word "codependent," often labeling people as codependent even when they are not. If you genuinely believe that you are codependent, speaking with an informed therapist is a great way to see if you genuinely align with the signs of a codependent individual.

You will not find any in-depth information as to what is officially classified as the symptoms of codependency, because it is not yet officially recognized as a distinctive disorder. However, most therapists who are educated on codependency and who have witnessed it in the individuals that they support have come to a common consensus as to what the hallmark traits of codependency are.

If you identify with any of the following statements, chances are you are experiencing symptoms of codependency:

- You have a tendency to want to rescue other people and may find yourself taking responsibility for them, even if you know you shouldn't.

- Whenever you sacrifice your own needs in favor of someone else's, you feel a sense of purpose. Sometimes, you will sacrifice your own needs to an extreme level, and you feel a boost to your self-esteem as a result.

- You regularly find yourself entering relationships where you will need to care for or even rescue the other individual, regardless of what it costs you. You are willing to invest high amounts of money, time, or other resources into taking care of others.

- You find yourself often attempting to resolve other people's conflicts, especially if their conflicts are related to addictions or chronic mental health, despite these troubles often being beyond your means to fix.

- Although you do not fully understand why, you seem to continually attract low-functioning people who are seeking caregivers to avoid having to take on adult responsibilities or consequences. Alternatively, you might regularly attract people who appear to be in perpetual crisis, yet who are unwilling to make any significant changes to their lives.

- It seems as though you regularly engage in behaviors that have the right intentions, but that come off as unproductive or unhealthy. An example of these behaviors would be enabling.

If you recognize these statements and feel as though they resonate with who you are and how you behave with and around others, chances are that you are experiencing codependency in your life. You can also look into your childhood to see if there are any indicating factors that may signal codependency or something that could potentially trigger the onset of codependency. If you lived a life where you had to suppress your own needs and wants to serve someone else growing up, chances are that you may be carrying that tendency into your adulthood in the form of codependency.

Inner Feelings of Codependents

The signs of codependency extend beyond expressive behavioral patterns and link into how an individual feels about themselves and the world around them, too. If you are a codependent individual, chances are that you exhibit the aforementioned behaviors linked with a variety of inner symptoms reflecting how you feel about yourself and your beliefs about life.

If you resonate with the signs of codependency, it is a good idea to look a little deeper and uncover what inner beliefs or thought processes may exist underneath the surface that could be contributing to your codependency. These inner beliefs are often the same amongst those who experience codependent tendencies, so they can be summarized in a few statements.

If you identify with any of these beliefs or experiences, chances are that you are experiencing symptoms of codependency:

- It is often hard for you to determine what it is that you want or need, so you struggle to make decisions or speak up for yourself.

- When you are in a relationship, you find yourself regularly doing what the other person wants and you genuinely feel that this is what you want, too. You do not spend any time considering how your wants or needs may vary from the other person's.

- You regularly experience difficulties with communication because you struggle to uncover exactly what it is that you are thinking or feeling. Sometimes, you simply say nothing because you don't know what to say or how to say it.

- Valuing yourself is challenging. You tend to value the approval of other people more than you value yourself in general.

- It is difficult for you to trust in yourself and in your abilities. You have a poor sense of self-esteem.

- You may experience severe fears of abandonment or neglect from others. This fear may be so extensive that you experience an obsessive need to be approved by others. Often, this fear gives you feelings of anxiety.

- When you are in a relationship, you find yourself heavily depending on that relationship. It is challenging for you to be in a relationship and see yourself as an individual both inside and outside of that relationship.

- You often find yourself taking responsibility for other people's actions. You may do so in a way that assumes the blame and allows them to blame you, or you may do so in a way that feels as though you can manipulate them into behaving a certain way if you change your own behaviors.

- Enforcing boundaries between yourself and others is challenging for you. You often find yourself overstepping other people's boundaries, while also allowing them to overstep yours.

- You may struggle to feel intimate with other people.

- You struggle to discern the difference between love and pity, and often find yourself feeling love for people whom you pity.

- When you are taking care of others, you find yourself constantly giving more than you get. When people do not recognize your selflessness, you feel hurt because, to you, this is your way of showing them love and it is not being appreciated or reciprocated.

- You seem to have a great deal of anger bottled up inside of you, but you may not know how to express it or utilize it. Instead, you keep it bottled up.

Sometimes, it may "spill out" and result in episodes of rage. If it does, you find yourself doing everything you can to make up for it.

- It may come naturally to you to lie or be dishonest with others, and it shows up in many ways. You may lie about your feelings, or how much you really do to take care of others or other things. Often, you believe these lies are for the greater good.

- Anytime you attempt to assert your needs in a conversation, you find yourself feeling incredibly guilty. In most cases, you attempt to avoid asserting your needs unless you absolutely have to, and even then, you find yourself holding off.

- In relationships, you find yourself holding on tight to avoid losing that relationship. You may find yourself going to extreme lengths to ensure that the other person won't leave you. You may also feel as though you cannot trust the other person not to leave, so you feel a regular state of anxiety. (This ties in with a fear of abandonment or neglect.)

- You may or may not realize it, but inside, you genuinely believe that you do not have rights, that your needs to do not matter and that you cannot have access to the love and affection that you crave.

- You are in denial about your behaviors and beliefs. You may even find yourself denying any of the behaviors or traits that you have read on this very list.

Psychologists who have dealt with individuals who experience codependency typically agree that the individual experiencing codependency struggles to identify themselves as an independent person. Often, they lack independence and have a severe inability to experience life as a their own person.

They find themselves jumping into unhealthy relationships with low-functioning people as a way to fill their need to become a caretaker and feel important and purposeful in life. In many instances, these unhealthy relationships lead to even lower feelings of self-worth and self-importance, which further reinforces the habits of codependency.

Examples of Codependent Behaviors

The actual expressive behaviors of a codependent individual are often tied in with a variety of different emotional reactions and responses. Because codependency can lead to things like anxiety, depression, excessive stress, and anger, it is likely that the actions of a codependent individual will reflect both traits of codependency as well as traits of these other potentially resulting emotional states.

Simply reading a list may not feel extensive enough for you to begin identifying symptoms of codependency within yourself. This is likely also linked to the tendency of not wanting to admit to your actions, likely out of guilt or shame for how they have impacted you and those around you.

Below, are three examples of codependency showing up in relationships and what these relationships actually look like from a codependent perspective. One relationship is based on a parent-child relationship, one is spousal, and one is for a child-parent relationship. Note that codependency can arise in any relationship, but according to the 2014 study by Bortolon, Barros, and Ferigolo, these are the most likely relationships for codependency to occur.

Example of a Codependent Child

If you were a codependent child, chances were your codependency was learned as a result of not having access to the resources required to fill your needs. This often happens when a child lives with a parent who is low-functioning, addicted, chronically mentally ill, or abusive. As a result of their parents' inability to fulfill their psychological, emotional, and sometimes physical needs, children become codependent as a way of having their needs filled.

Let's say, for the sake of this example, that you are experiencing codependency as a child because your parent is abusive. Chances are that any time you express a need, the fulfillment of the need is withheld from you. Sometimes, in addition to withholding it, your parent also shames you or makes you feel guilty for having that need.

As a child, it is your parents' responsibility to recognize your needs and support you in fulfilling them since you are not yet capable of doing so yourself. However, because your needs are not being fulfilled and, in some cases, you are being shamed for even having them, you begin to believe that your needs are not important and that you are not capable of having them fulfilled.

Over time, you realize that this parent is not going to fulfill your needs, yet the need doesn't actually go away. In fact, the need persists and your unconscious mind continues looking for opportunities to have that need fulfilled. As a result, it begins searching for ways that you can appeal to the person responsible for fulfilling your needs in hopes of having that need met. This often manifests in a people-pleasing codependent archetype within the child.

As a way to get your needs met, you begin doing everything the way that you believe the other person wants it to be done. You also begin desperately searching for approval, which is what you use to determine whether or not you are effectively appealing to the person who regularly withholds from you the fulfillment of your needs. When you do receive this approval, you translate that into acceptance and love, and you continue behaving in the way that grants you approval from the other person, even if it seems unreasonable or requires you to sacrifice yourself.

Alternatively, if you do not acquire approval, you likely take it personally and find yourself feeling extremely hurt. This is because you are desperately trying to prove that you are worthy of love and acceptance, and without validation or approval from someone else, you struggle to hold that belief within yourself. Those very feelings of unworthiness and dissatisfaction that lead to you partaking in people-pleasing behaviors are triggered and, once again, the trauma of being unworthy is reinforced within you.

Often, these types of codependent experiences go on to affect an individual well into adulthood. In order for an individual who was codependent as a child to go on and experience freedom from codependent behaviors as an adult, they require therapy to support them in discovering why they began behaving codependently in the first place. Through this therapy, they can heal from their childhood experiences and begin learning how to implement healthy systems in their relationships between themselves and others.

Example of a Codependent Spouse

Often, spousal codependency results when one person was conditioned to be accepting of codependent experiences in childhood. This could be because they were codependent as a child, or because they were never taught to see themselves as independent and worthy. As a result, their low self-esteem and low self-confidence leave them vulnerable to entering unhealthy relationships that may or may not result in codependency later in life.

In a codependent relationship with a spouse, the dynamic is challenging. In this particular relationship, you feel a sense of devotion to your partner because you love them and see them as your equal in life. However, what ends up happening is that the "functional" partner in the relationship becomes overcommitted to the "unhealthy" partner. As a result of this over commitment, the once-functional partner no longer cares about themselves because they desire to care for and potentially even "fix" the other partner.

In codependent relationships amongst spouses, the most common codependent archetype to arise is the martyr because the codependent partner wants to help the other partner. In the end, the codependent person is the one who struggles or suffers, not the unhealthy partner in the relationship.

This is because, in most cases, the unhealthy partner is unwilling or unable to admit their unhealthy ways and so, they will not or cannot seek out the proper treatments to fix themselves. The codependent will constantly adjust and readjust their own needs and actions to attempt to fix the other person only to realize that nothing ever actually works. As a result, they experience a severe amount of stress and discomfort.

Most people find themselves questioning why the codependent individual does not simply leave and find themselves a newer and healthier relationship. The reality is that this typically does not happen and there are far too many reasons as to why it never happens.

In many cases, psychologists do not yet entirely understand why the individual does not leave, either.

The three most common answers that psychologists reach are abuse, fear of abandonment or neglect, or childhood grooming. If the codependent partner is being abused in any way, they may find themselves too afraid to leave for fear of what might happen if they do. Alternatively, if the codependent partner experienced trauma relating to abandonment or neglect in their childhood or if they were raised as a codependent child, they may already be vulnerable to this relationship dynamic.

Example of a Codependent Parent

Parents have a natural inner need to care for their children and make sure that they are well. This is likely why parents are one of the groups that are most vulnerable to developing codependent tendencies. As a parent, you want to make sure that your kid is safe and has everything that they need. For some parents, however, there is a point where being the caregiver turns into being a codependent parent.

When you are codependent upon your child, it can lead to many challenging dynamics. Psychologists have uncovered that one of the most common reasons why parents become codependent is because they feel a sense of obligation to their child and, if they perceive that this obligation is not being fulfilled, they feel guilty. This leads to them feeling as though they cannot make any other decisions except to be there for their child.

Typically, mothers are the more likely to become codependent, though fathers can certainly become codependent on their children, too. Codependent parenting often stems from feelings of guilt, such as if you were absent for most of your child's life, or if your child suffered a trauma such as abuse or rape that you felt you were unable to protect them from. It is especially common in parents who give birth to children who struggle to engage in normal behaviors as a result of physical or mental disabilities.

In some cases, a child may be exploiting the parent's codependent behaviors by using it as an opportunity to avoid having to take responsibility for themselves and their own actions. In others, the child may not have any choice because they are physically or mentally unable to understand the unhealthy dynamic of the relationship and contribute to it in a healthier manner.

Parents who are codependent to otherwise healthy children often find themselves taking extensive care of their child, far beyond what their child actually needs. In some cases, codependent parents will prevent the child from expressing independence or individuality so they can keep the child feeling as though they require the care and attention of the parent. It is not uncommon to see children being sheltered and excessively tended to when a parent is codependent because, unconsciously, the parent is attempting to avoid losing the child. By leaving them ill-equipped to deal with the world and face life as an independent adult, the parent can continue to feel needed and important.

In situations where codependent parents reach that state as a result of having a disabled child, this can be especially challenging on the parent, as their feelings of guilt leave them feeling as though there is no alternative. They may feel hopeless and trapped, and they may exhibit codependent behaviors because their obligation to their child is all they have come to know.

In many cases, codependent parents with disabled children experience feelings of isolation as they have become so codependent upon their children that they cannot successfully interact with other healthily functioning adults. As a result, their friendships and romantic relationships may suffer in favor of their need to care for their child. This can be both a symptom of codependency, and a factor that makes codependency worse in these unique circumstances.

The 5 Codependent Archetypes

Not every person who experiences codependency exhibits it in the exact same manner. Although the core driving forces behind their behaviors seem to be the same, there are various ways in which an individual will exhibit their codependency and use it as a way to get their needs met.

According to Lauren Zander, a psychologist who founded "The Handel Method," as humans, we unconsciously assign everyone in our lives a role. We then mentally devise strategies for how we are going to deal with these people based on who they are and what they need or want from us.

She claims that, as humans, we do not realize that we are mentally directing and manipulating people and the situations that we experience with them based on the opinions that we have already formulated on these individuals. Expanding on this theory, certified addictions professional, Dr. Jamie Huysman, claims that the roles we believe that ourselves and others play are often passed down through generations. This means that we integrate the roles taught to us both verbally and expressively from our parents and other influential family members who taught us how to treat others and how to let them treat us.

In unhealthy familial relationships, the roles that are taught to us often reflect unhealthy standards and unhealthy boundaries. For codependent individuals, this can lead to them experiencing what are known as "codependent archetypes" that distinguish how they will think and behave in various relationships. A codependent person can adjust which archetype they play from relationship to relationship, and they can also play multiple archetypes in a single relationship depending on what is needed in that present moment.

The following subsections discuss the six primary archetypes of codependents in greater detail. These six include the martyr, the savior, the adviser, the caregiver, the people pleaser, and the yes-person. These archetypes have been explained with expertise offered by aforementioned psychologists Zander, Huysman, and their fellow psychologist, Julie Sullivan.

The "Martyr"

As the martyr, you have a tendency to put other's needs ahead of your own to the point that you now experience suffering from your own actions. At some point, you were taught that sacrificing yourself in favor of fulfilling others' needs is virtuous, and so, that is exactly what you do. You might notice that you are the type of person to give up on your own needs or desires to fulfill someone else's.

Some of the common action taken by the martyr includes paying for yourself and your friends even when you cannot afford it or taking on extra tasks at work that you cannot reasonably handle. You may also find yourself skipping out on engaging in your own personal activities, such as going to the gym or spending time with a friend, in favor of spending time with the person that you tend to be codependent towards.

In platonic relationships, as a codependent martyr, you likely find yourself giving up on everything in order to serve the other person's needs. This can result in you giving up your intimate relationships, flaking out on your hobbies, and failing to nurture other friendships in favor of what the other person needs.

For example, say you have a friend who is particularly needy and say that their date canceled on them, so they call you and request that you come to support them and keep them from spending the night alone. If you were a codependent martyr, you would give up your plans for the night and go spend time with them, even if you had something important planned like a date of your own. This can result in you resenting this friend because you are constantly running to be with them and are repeatedly sacrificing yourself and your own resources in order to do so.

In romantic relationships, you will behave similarly to how you do in platonic relationships. However, because you are in a romantic relationship, you may find yourself giving up even more. For example, if you move in together, you may take responsibility for everything involved in the process of living together, from cleaning to running errands and everything in between.

You may sacrifice your time, desires, and needs to make sure that the household is maintained and everyone has their needs filled on a daily basis. If your partner needs anything, you will likely drop everything to make sure that your partner's needs are met and that they do not have to fulfill their needs on their own.

The problem with being a martyr is that through sacrificing yourself, you end up neglecting yourself and your needs. You neglect the process of showing yourself love, acceptance, and approval, in favor of seeking it from others through your acts of selflessness. In the end, you begin resenting those whom you have helped because they rarely return the favor, they take you for granted, or they begin to resent you, too.

As a codependent martyr, it is likely that you do not fully recognize how your own actions teach others to treat you. You may believe that excessive acts of selflessness and obsessively caring for others is a sign of love, thus leaving you feeling that the love is not being reciprocated when people do not act the same way with you.

It may also feel like you genuinely cannot meet your own needs because you feel guilty trying, or more likely because you experience an intense nagging in your mind that pressures you to fulfill someone else's needs or desires first. These behaviors have become so habitual to you that they are picked up by your unconscious mind and you likely do not even recognize when they are happening or how they are contributing to your unhealthy relationships.

It is imperative that anyone behaving with the archetype of the martyr learns how they can begin distinguishing the differences between selfishness and self-care. Learning to put yourself first and put others second allows you to begin taking care of yourself, and understanding that through doing this, you are not being rude or inconsiderate towards the other person.

The reality is that, in most cases, no one will go without if you choose to focus on tending to your own needs first and then tending to everyone else's second. Instead, you will have more energy and feel better about yourself, and the acts that you fulfill for other people will feel more sincere and will not come with such heavy expectations on how they should treat you in return.

The "Savior"

As the savior, you believe that it is your responsibility to save the day and prevent people from hurting themselves or others in the big dangerous world. Anytime someone you know finds themselves in a troubling situation, you are always the one there bailing them out and protecting them from having to face their own consequences.

You lend your friends money when they need it (even if they don't pay you back), and you are there trying to fix your friend's broken heart every time another miserable relationship falls apart. You may even find yourself attracting people who seem to constantly be dealing with chaos and struggle or who have severe issues with addictions and you find yourself always jumping out to rescue them.

In a platonic relationship, as the codependent savior, you likely find yourself spending time with friends who seem to have nothing going for them and use this as an opportunity to fulfill your need to "save the day." You may be surrounded by people who struggle to hold a job, who are unable to make productive choices for themselves and their future, and who are emotionally needy. This lets you feel as though you can be there for them and save them so that they do not fall victim to the world around them. In saving them, you fulfill your own need of being needed by those around you.

In a romantic relationship, you likely find yourself attached to people who are especially ill-equipped to live on their own and make productive decisions for themselves. By choosing someone who repeatedly makes poor decisions, or someone who truly cannot make *positive* decisions, you give yourself the perfect opportunity to have long-term access to someone who will need your saving.

You then spend that time finding ways to save them from every trouble they may get themselves into, no matter what it costs you. You will fight their battles, pay their bail, and lick their wounds if it means that you get to save them from their own pain or consequences.

The problem with being the savior is that you go from lending a helping hand to trying to be the cure for everyone else's problems. Instead of offering reasonable amounts of help, you overextend your hand and may even find yourself taking on repercussions or consequences from someone else's actions.

Not only does this generate a significant amount of stress for you from being an enabler, but it also prevents the person who you are sharing this codependent relationship with from growing. They never have to endure the consequences of their own actions, so they never seem to learn and the cycle continues until one of you finds a way to break it.

When you are experiencing the position of the savior, it is essential that you begin to focus on gaining some perspective within your relationships. The best way is to focus on your relationships, especially the one that involves the person you are codependent with, and ask yourself what you want for that person.

Do you really want them to have to rely on you for everything and lack the competency to handle things on their own? Or do you want them to feel empowered to make their own decisions and confident that they can handle these decisions accordingly? If your desire for them is to have them feeling empowered and confident, you need to learn to step back and give them the space to learn how to do things on their own. It is not your job to do everything for them, so while you can certainly lend a hand, do not be afraid to outright refuse to help them in some circumstances. This will teach them to do it on their own.

If you find that the reason why you are playing savior is that you want to feel needed and valued in your relationships, it is important that you take the time to recognize this motivation and find healthier ways to fulfill it. In these conditions, getting the outside perspective of a therapist can support you in seeing the areas of yourself and your relationships that are not easily apparent to you. That way, you can get a clearer understanding of why you are feeling unvalued and how you can begin to fulfill that need in a healthier manner.

The "Adviser"

People who are codependent with the adviser archetype are likely involved in a relationship where both partners are engaging in a practice known as "borrowed functioning." This means that one person is taking charge as a way to attempt to control the situation so that they can feel fulfilled, and one person is being taken control of as a way to feel fulfilled. For both people, their sense of self-confidence and self-esteem is low, so they depend on each other to have their needs fulfilled.

If you are the adviser, chances are that you find yourself constantly looking into other people's lives and giving them advice, even if it hasn't been asked for. In most cases, you are likely giving advice and putting pressure on them to follow that advice rather than simply giving them the freedom to make their own decisions.

This leads to your advice becoming more of a rule or a command than a recommendation, which results in the said person feeling as though they have to follow through. If they allow you to engage in this type of controlling behavior, chances are that they are dealing with similar issues of codependency but it is manifesting in an entirely different way for them.

In platonic relationships, as an adviser, you are likely very pushy towards your friends. You may seek to surround yourself with people who lack confidence and drive, and then you superimpose on their lives by pushing your advice onto them and pressuring them to take it. It may feel as though you are constantly pushing them along and nagging at them to achieve their "next level," yet they never fully do because they are not actually doing it for themselves.

This can lead to a small feeling of success every time someone takes your advice and it goes well, but a massive feeling of disappointment every time the advice does not hold up for long because they did not truly care. It can also lead to you feeling overburdened by your friends because you feel as though you have to constantly push them forward and they never seem to have any drive themselves.

In romantic relationships, you likely have a tendency to get together with people who have virtually no drive to accomplish anything in life. This drive could be for any number of reasons, including low self-esteem, low self-confidence, or simply a lack of motivation. In these relationships, you attempt to use your advice and pressure as a way to push your partner to achieve their fullest potential, which they never seem to do.

This can begin to feel overwhelming because you may feel as though you want to see more come of the relationship (and your controlling actions), but you never do. Your unwillingness to give the other person space and let them be their own person, as well as their own lack of desire, result in them not advancing in any particular direction and you feeling stressed out and like you are constantly dragging them along.

The problem with being the adviser is that when you are overly invested in another person's decisions, you have breached their "force field." Their force field is symbolic of their personal space—their sense of individuality and self—and their ability to engage in life in a way that exhibits that sense of self.

When you breach it, you essentially take control and hijack that person's ability to engage in life independently so to speak. If it has effectively happened, the person whose force field you have breached has allowed you to do so, likely because they have not been taught about how to confidently be independent and make their own choices.

In this situation, it is unlikely that the other person is going to begin enforcing healthy boundaries for you to begin adhering to. Instead, you need to take the time to discover what healthy boundaries are and to begin respecting them with this person as well as anyone else in your life. At first, both sides are likely to experience some degree of distress from this type of change since you were both benefitting from the exchange.

However, as you begin to adhere to healthy boundaries, you offer yourself the opportunity to let go of control and give the other person the space required to begin learning how to take control over their own lives. Then, your relationship can be reframed with a mutual respect.

The "People Pleaser"

As a people pleaser, you love having other people praise you and show you an appreciation for the things you do for them. Whenever someone needs help or requires something, you are more than happy to oblige and support them in any way that you can.

You likely even find yourself behaving differently around different people or even lying about who you truly are so that other people like you and offer you the opportunity to help them when they need it. Then, through helping them or joining them in their activities, you seek their praise and approval by going above and beyond to be the best that you can be. In fact, you may even resonate with the term "perfectionist."

In platonic relationships, you likely find yourself exhausted by your friends, yet still constantly showing up and trying to impress them. It is likely that you are the one always offering to host dinner parties or arrange plans for everyone and that you extend yourself above and beyond to attempt to make every gathering next-level.

Whenever people express a lack of appreciation for what you have done, you likely take it personally and try to make the next gathering even better. You exhaust yourself trying to outdo yourself and give other people reasons to appreciate you, so your platonic friendships feel more like chores than positive relationships.

In romantic relationships, as a people pleaser, you likely find yourself incredibly exhausted. If you are living together, this can be even worse. It is likely that you find yourself constantly listening to everything your partner says they like, and attempting to mold yourself to fit the image of everything you think your partner wants so that you become the "perfect partner."

You hope that this will make them love and appreciate you more. When your partner doesn't show you this increased sense of appreciation, you may end up feeling neglected or unloved because you thought your actions would earn you a greater appreciation than what that person can reasonably offer.

The problem with being a people pleaser is that your need to do things for others and gain praise from them is obsessive. When you do not gain the praise or appreciation that you were hoping for, you begin feeling depressed or personally attacked because the other person didn't notice you. In most cases, the other person did not realize that you needed or wanted appreciation or recognition which leads to the lack thereof, thus resulting in you taking it personally when it was never meant to be a personal attack.

You might also find yourself feeling as if the things that should bring you joy are burdensome because you have to put in so much work just to get appreciation from others. The constant over performing just to get some recognition is exhausting, so in many cases, you feel overwhelmed by and resentful of doing what should be fun things like hosting dinner parties or having company over because you do not want to put the energy in. Still, you do it because you desperately crave the attention and approval of other people.

If your people-pleasing tendencies developed as a child, which many do, it is likely that you can recall outright asking for the approval of others in your youth. It is not uncommon for people-pleasing children to repeatedly ask things like "Is this good enough?" "Do you like this?" "Did I do well?" and other questions that are directly aimed towards receiving approval in return.

When it comes to being a people pleaser, the best thing you can do is learn how to begin saying no and not volunteering yourself for things that you genuinely do not want to partake in. If you are unsure as to when you should start saying no, you should begin focusing on asking yourself the following questions about every offer:

- "Does this choice make me feel filled up or empty?"

- "Will I truly be rejected if I say no?"

- "How do I feel in my body when I imagine saying yes? How about when I imagine saying no?"

These questions will help you begin to understand whether or not the decisions you are making are actually right for you. When you make choices more consciously, it stops you from trying to do everything and be everything for everyone. Plus, when you say no to the things that do not fill you up or make you feel happy, you can begin saying yes to the things that truly light you up and make you feel great.

The "Yes-Person"

If you are the type of person that says yes then later resents it because you meant no, then you are a "yes person." Yes people pretend to agree with others and plaster a smile on their face even if they disagree because they fear saying what they genuinely feel. As a yes person, you are unlikely to voice your opinions that are different from someone else's because you do not want to create conflict. In your mind, experiencing conflict with someone else can result in you not having your needs met and so you feel as though you have to remain in constant agreement with people even if you do not actually agree.

In platonic relationships, being a yes-person means that you likely have a hard time being around many people because the act of agreeing with everyone and trying to avoid conflict can be challenging. You may feel exhausted after gatherings with your friends, especially if they are opinionated, because you struggle to express your own opinions and speak the truth.

You likely feel like you are wearing a mask and like none of your friends truly know who you are because you have never been able to honestly express yourself and your opinions to them. As a result, you may feel incredibly lonely, and struggle with feelings of depression relating to these isolating experiences.

In romantic relationships, you likely feel quite similar. However, because romantic relationships tend to be more intimate in nature, you likely find yourself feeling even more exhausted. As an attempt to seek approval from your partner, chances are you never disagree with them and you find yourself doing many things that you do not particularly enjoy.

You likely experience both isolation and shame because it feels like your partner does not truly know who you are, and that can be challenging. When they inevitably catch glimpses of who you truly are, you may then begin feeling ashamed of yourself for not successfully upholding the image that you have been pretending to portray. This constant attempt at holding up a mask can lead to severe problems with intimacy in your romantic relationships.

The biggest problem with a yes person is that they never voice their needs or opinions separate from someone else's. As a result, they end up feeling a deep sense of resentment towards other people because they feel as though they are not allowed to have their own opinion.

Any time they experience these feelings of resentment or frustration, they avoid facing them and instead bottle them in. In the end, they end up extremely unhappy and unclear as to how they can effectively deal with these emotions in a way that is compassionate and constructive.

The focus in overcoming the archetype of the yes person is learning how to begin speaking your truth. This process can be slow as, oftentimes, people of this type do not even realize what their actual truth even is. Alternatively, they may know exactly what their truth is, but they fear that voicing it could result in some form of negative consequences, so they avoid it altogether and instead hold on to the resentment and unfulfilled needs.

The first step for the yes person to begin speaking their truth is to begin building an understanding of what their truth is, and building the courage to recognize it and voice it. You also need to learn that speaking your truth does not mean that you have to be confrontational or argumentative.

You can speak your truth in a way that exhibits compassion and empathy towards the other person while still expressing your thoughts or needs. Learning effective communication styles and feeling confident in your communication is imperative if you want to stop stuffing your emotions down and saying yes even if you don't mean it.

CHAPTER 3: ARE YOU IN A CODEPENDENT RELATIONSHIP?

Codependency in relationships is a really painful thing to endure, and it can result in a lot of negative psychological and emotional side effects for both the codependent partner and the person upon whom they are codependent. As the term "codependency" continues to grow and be understood, one major drawback is that many people are falsely accusing others of being codependent when, in fact, they are not. This leads to confusion in what codependency is and how it actually impacts relationships.

According to therapist and published author Shannon Thomas, codependency generally creeps into relationships early on and can slowly begin to grow as the codependent partner requires more and more to feel satisfied. From what she has seen and understood, most relationships do not actually start out as codependent.

Instead, they typically start out with normal interactions, and then move towards codependency when the codependent partner does not get what they expected they would from the encounter. For example, if the other person starts pulling back, the codependent will begin assuming the full responsibility of reaching out to connect with the other partner. This is how they work to keep the gap bonded and prevent the relationship from ending so that they can continue to get their needs filled by this person.

If you have recognized signs of codependency in yourself and are now wondering if you are experiencing codependency in your relationships, with the help of research and findings from various psychologists, doctors, and experts, this chapter will support you in determining if it really is codependency that is impacting your relationship.

Realize that this codependency can show up in any relationship in your life, which means that you may recognize these behaviors showing up even in an unlikely situation, such as with a coworker. You should also understand that you are likely to recognize some of these behaviors in multiple relationships that you also keep since codependents tend to treat everyone in a fairly similar way. However, there will likely be only one person that you experience virtually all of these symptoms with, which is the person that you are most dependent on.

Signs of Codependency in Relationships

According to Tracy Malone, therapist and founder of Narcissistic Abuse Support, codependency often becomes apparent when the codependent realizes that they are trying to "fix" the other person. This often results in the codependent displaying classic symptoms of the savior archetype, where they try to rescue the other partner and help them experience a better life.

Often, this desire to save the other person in the relationship arises because the codependent has entered the relationship assuming that the other person would take on a specific role. When they didn't, the codependent became upset and felt that they could not genuinely feel fulfilled unless that person lived up to their expectations, so they begin trying to "fix" the other person as a way to have their needs met.

When a codependent partner begins trying to "fix" their partner, it shows a lack of respect for who they are and a lack of trust in their partner's ability to be a whole and complete person. This leads to a changed dynamic in the relationship where the codependent begins unconsciously manipulating the other person to feel incomplete by attempting to shift them into their chosen role for that person. It can also result in the codependent investing so much time into the relationship that they no longer have the desire to take care of themselves and consider their own needs.

Another common symptom of codependent relationships is when the codependent partner immediately drops all of their boundaries to serve the other person. UK-Based psychologist and executive coach Perpetua Neo, an expert in toxic relationships, claims that many codependent partners will completely drop their own boundaries and fully devote to serving their partner no matter what the cost is.

When a codependent partner completely drops their boundaries in favor of the other person, they give up their own story and give more credit to their partner's story. This value that a codependent places on their partner's story exceeds the value they place upon themselves and supports them in attempting to write themselves into someone else's narrative to have their own needs met. The codependent will completely write off their own right to having a life that is independent of the other person, and the other person's right to the same, to attempt to fulfill their needs, which leads us to our next point.

Dating coach Erika Ettin points out that most codependent partners struggle to see themselves as independent of their partner, so they struggle to live their own separate life. Chances are that the codependent partner will want to do everything with the other person and stay as involved as possible in their lives. They may avoid picking up their own hobbies or doing things on their own because they genuinely feel as though they cannot do anything alone or without their partner.

Unfortunately, in giving up this individuality, the codependent ultimately loses their sense of personal identity and begins trying to mesh themselves into the other person's life. In other words, they truly do not know who they are and they struggle to be and feel like a complete person all on their own.

One of the most challenging signs that you are in a codependent relationship is if you begin losing contact with people who are important to you, such as your family. According to psychotherapist Dr. Jonathan Marshall, in his work, he has witnessed many codependents who begin to lose contact with other people who matter to them in favor of maintaining a relationship with the person upon whom they are dependent.

As a result, when they realize that the relationship is not a good fit, they have nowhere to turn and end up feeling isolated and alone. This can result in codependents staying in a toxic relationship for a long time, waiting for the resources to make a change and do something better for themselves. They fear that if they leave, they have no alternative life to go to.

If you find yourself constantly looking to your partner for the approval to do things, chances are that you are in a codependent relationship according to author Catenya McHenry. Through her writing, where she shares her personal experience of being married to a narcissist, Catenya realized that one major sign of codependency is having to look to your partner for approval on everything. This is because a codependent does not feel as though they are capable of making their own decisions, and they want to please their partner.

So, they hope that by searching for approval on everything, they can get the validation they need, which helps the codependent feel fulfilled and good about themselves. Codependents struggle to realize that they are capable of making their own decisions and often attempt to make decisions alongside their partner, claiming it is common courtesy and not necessarily a dependency. This exhibits their tendency to lean towards denial when it comes to admitting that they are doing something that reflects codependent behavior.

Lastly, according to NYC-based psychologist and writer Elinor Greenberg, Phd, a common factor in codependent relationships is having the partner who is not codependent have some form of unhealthy behavioral mannerism. If your partner repeatedly engages in unhealthy behaviors, such as binge drinking, aggressively asserting their emotions, or taking drugs, the chances of the relationship involving codependency are heightened. In some cases, it may even encourage the codependent to begin engaging in these unhealthy behaviors because they lack the inner boundaries required to refrain from engaging in them, even if they know better.

Symptoms of a Codependent Relationship

While we just discovered many signs that indicate that codependency is occurring in a relationship, there are far more than the ones that we just discussed. Below are additional symptoms that a codependent relationship may face, either directly as a result of codependency or as a side effect of other issues codependency can cause. These symptoms are the commonly agreed upon side effects proposed by the psychology community as a whole.

- Outside of your codependent relationship, it is hard for you to genuinely engage in other activities and feel satisfaction or happiness from these activities.

- You continue to stay even if the relationship appears to be toxic or an ill-fit match and you may not know exactly why.

- When it comes to your partner, you will do absolutely anything for them no matter what it means for you. In the past, you have done things like put off seeing family and friends, getting involved in hobbies or activities, or even furthering your career so that you can be available to this person.

- In your relationship, you feel a constant sense of anxiety. This anxiety is sometimes related to your fear of not doing enough to make the other person happy, and is sometimes related to your fear of losing the other person.

- It is not unusual for you to invest what others might consider to be an excessive amount of time in serving the needs of your partner and making sure that they receive everything they have ever asked for.

- When it comes to expressing your own needs in the relationship, you feel guilty and will often avoid doing so because you do not want to be a burden on your partner. Sometimes, you even feel guilty just for thinking about your needs, even though they have not yet been expressed.

- Sometimes, in your relationship, you ignore your own inner morals or values to do what the other person wants to do.

- It is not uncommon for you to feel feelings of shame or low self-esteem in your relationship. You worry that you are not good enough or deserving enough of having what you want or even having what you already have.

- You may feel as though you are easily triggered by your partner, sometimes becoming excessively defensive or angry because you immediately absorb other people's thoughts and words. It is hard for you not to take things personally because you take everything in so deeply.

- If your partner needs something and you do not begin making it happen, you feel extremely guilty and it is hard for you to think about doing anything else.

- You may find yourself being controlling in relationships, sometimes, trying to control other people to get them to act, think, or behave in the way you have told them to. To you, this keeps everything orderly and sane and prevents any chaos from prevailing in your world.

- It may feel like you are constantly thinking about the other person to the point that you are somewhat obsessive about them and the relationship that you share. You may even find yourself obsessing over interactions you shared, trying to see what you did right or wrong, and attempting to find a way to do better next time.

- If you begin to feel as though you are being rejected, you may find that you have an exaggerated reaction to this experience. You may find yourself completely withdrawing, feeling deep and immense sadness, or even becoming extremely angry and hostile for those feelings of rejection.

- When it comes to sex, you may experience either a need to have a lot of it or a tendency to push away from it in relationships if it is a relationship that is sexual in nature. If you require plenty, chances are you use sex as a way to feel approval from others. If you tend to avoid it, you may be attempting to avoid the shame or rejection that could arise from the experience.

- With general intimacy in relationships, you may struggle to be open and honest with those around you about your inner world for fear of them judging you and leaving you. You may also excessively open up and over explain yourself as a way to seek approval and acceptance for the feelings you have inside.

- As a result of all of these symptoms, you may regularly struggle with feelings of resentment, anger, anxiety, and depression. Sometimes, if the feelings become too much, you may even find yourself experiencing numbness to the world around you.

- As you read through these, you may find yourself attempting to deny that any of this takes place in your relationship or that it is causing the damage that it truly is. Even though some, or all, of these behaviors may appear to be relatable, you might be trying to rationalize your behaviors and justify why you do things to such an extreme level.

Types of Codependent Relationships

As you know, codependency was originally used as a term that described individuals who shared close relationships with alcoholics, often to the point of interference in an alcoholic or addict's ability to recover. However, codependency has now become recognized as a common trait that occurs in three different types of relationships: those involving addictions, those involving abuse, and those involving a "fear of man."

Codependency can also arise in a previous relationship and carry over into future relationships when the codependent partner has not been able to fully recover in between relationships. As a result, the relationship is exhibiting codependency but it may not necessarily be doing so in an obvious circumstance of addiction, abuse, or fear of man. However, those in the relationship will still be experiencing a dysfunctional dynamic that was designed to foster and support the behaviors of the codependent individual.

Relationships That Involve Addiction

In relationships that involve addiction, a dynamic arises that involves feelings of infidelity. Although the addicted partner may not actually be engaging in inappropriate intimate relationships with other people, their primary affection is granted to someone other than their partner.

What ends up happening is that this partner lies, threatens, pleads, silences, and betrays their partner over and over, causing feelings of mistrust and fear in the other person. As a result, the partner who is receiving the mistreatment from the addict can develop codependency as they continue to attempt to have their needs met within the relationship from someone who is incapable of meeting those needs.

Often, codependent individuals involved in relationships with an addict will use codependency as a way to accommodate for the "other" that exists in the relationship, in this case, the drugs, to attempt to keep some form of order in the relationship. Over time, this ability to accommodate for the substance that is being abused becomes increasingly unhealthy and results in codependency.

Relationships That Involve Abuse

In relationships that involve abuse, an imbalance of power is present that results in codependent behaviors arising in the relationship. In these circumstances, the abuse is often done in an intermittent manner that creates the illusion that it is not truly a major issue. The codependent person may also experience gaslighting as a way to pressure them into believing that the abusive partner was not to blame and that it was the codependent partner's fault that the encounter happened.

A common and very realistic example of this is in the dynamic that exists between narcissists and individuals who become codependent. In these relationships, often perfectly healthy and capable individuals become codependent as a result of the manipulation and psychological abuse.

When the abuse continues to grow, the codependent partner faces a myriad of problems that result in their codependency coming forward and creating issues in their lives. For example, the abusive behaviors lead them to feel ashamed and, oftentimes, isolate themselves from those around them for fear of being seen as weak, or worse, deserving of the abuse for staying for so long.

The abuse can also lead to codependents coping by finding ways to minimize or justify the abuse, thus leading to them staying in the unhealthy relationship even longer. In the end, a codependent partner in an abusive relationship will often stay because they fear that they cannot safely leave the relationship and even if they could, there would be nowhere and nothing to go to.

Relationships That Involve a "Fear of Man"

In some cases, a person is raised to fear what society will think of them and how they will be perceived by others around them so they never effectively learn to value their own opinions and beliefs. In these instances, an individual's personal fear of society and of being rejected or abandoned can lead to them entering relationships where they already have codependent behaviors prior to the relationship starting. This can lead to them entering relationships with dysfunctional or low-functioning people, or entering relationships that would have otherwise been healthy, but then sabotaging them to fit their ideas or expectations.

For the most part, this codependency arises from an inner belief system that is working against the individual as an ineffective way to attempt to protect them from the dangers of the world around them. They end up becoming codependent on the other person because they feel as though this is the one person who is safe for them and that the rest of society will not be there for them. So, they cling to this one person as a way to feel safe and have their needs met because they genuinely believe that the rest of society will not be helpful in making this happen.

The Negative Impact of Codependency for Both Parties

Codependency can have a negative impact on everyone involved, and can sometimes even result in individuals that are not involved in the relationship being impacted, too. A study done at University College Dublin in 1999 by James Cullen and Alan Carr revealed the major deficiencies and drawbacks in codependent relationships that affect both parties.

The areas of the relationships that were impacted by codependency involved roles, affective expression, communication, control, emotional involvement, and values and norms. It was also noted that a large percentage of individuals in highly codependent relationships were in a relationship involving an addict, likely making the instance of codependency even worse.

What they found, not surprisingly, was that the root cause of suffering for individuals in codependent relationships was that they were unable to feel independent of one another, especially in relationships that involved addiction. As a result, the codependent partner consistently tries to have their needs met by someone who can't meet them, often finding themselves trying to mold themselves and the other person into what they feel is required in order for their needs to be met.

The partner that is not codependent also suffers because they, too, do not see themselves as independent, and often take advantage of the codependent partner as a way to avoid having to do things for themselves. Instead, they can leave it up to the codependent partner who will do anything to please them, thus allowing them to step out of a role of responsibility and feel justified in passing off both responsibility and blame to the codependent partner.

The other significant finding of the study was that the unhealthy dynamic of the relationship is often recognized by one or both partners and both can typically identify multiple negative side effects that they experience as a result of the relationship. However, these unhealthy dynamics often lead to lower self-esteem and psychological problems (such as anxiety and depression) that lead to one or both partners feeling trapped in the relationship and like there is nowhere else for them to go.

Feeling like there is no way out leaves them trapped in this unhealthy dynamic where the cycle continues as both parties continue to feel worse about themselves and struggle to improve their lives in any significant way.

Addiction and Codependency

If addiction is at play in the relationship that you are experiencing codependency in, chances are that you may be wondering exactly how it comes into play and how it results in codependency developing in the non-addicted partner. Since codependency was originally discovered in Alcoholics Anonymous, the majority of resources continue to link codependency closely with addictions and individuals involved in relationships with addicts.

It is important to realize that, as cited in the study done by Cullen and Carr, just because addictions are present in a relationship, it does not guarantee that an individual is experiencing or definitely will experience codependency. Conversely, it does not mean that every codependent relationship has addiction at the center of it. Still, there are many ways in which addiction can encourage the development of codependency and it is important that you understand both how and why.

Over the years, psychologists have mutually agreed that codependency and addiction are likely linked through the fact that the addict has difficulties engaging in a healthy and normal lifestyle and the codependent feels obligated to take care of them. This leads to the codependent over compensating in care and doing more for the addict than is reasonable, often as a way to attempt to maintain a sense of calmness in the relationship.

Codependency often starts when an addict begins to exhibit issues with maintaining a job, earning a decent income, cultivating healthy relationships, engaging in high-risk behaviors or needing a constant source of emotional support. Typically, a spouse, parent, sibling, friend or even coworker will recognize these needs and offer support as a way to try and lift the addict out of a tough situation and give them the opportunity to do better. When the addict receives the support but fails to make a productive change with the support, they come back to that person in need of additional support.

In many cases, the addict will realize that the codependent individual is willing to help them out, and they will exploit this generosity and continue to come back, sometimes, even bullying the codependent into helping them again and again. The codependent continues helping, despite their better judgment, and eventually finds themselves feeling as though they cannot stop helping. It is not uncommon for the codependent to help out in ways that result in them missing out on things in their own lives, such as other relationships, financial wellbeing, a career, or anything else that may have come in the way of their ability to support the addict.

In the end, they suffer tremendously and the addict does, too. The codependent ends up taking all of the responsibility for both individuals and finds themselves feeling overwhelmed and overburdened, often resenting the addict but feeling too guilty to make a change. They may also feel ashamed for the amount that they have given and lost to the addict in the process of supporting them, potentially to the point of preventing them from reaching out for support.

The addict suffers because they are not being encouraged to take responsibility for their own actions, which ultimately results in them staying trapped in their addictive behaviors. Because they do not have to take responsibility and recognize the consequences of their actions, addicts become incapable of making a change because they do not feel the impact of their addictions and are being enabled by the codependent. As you can see, this is a lose-lose situation for both parties.

Part 2: Overcoming Codependency In Relationships

LEAH CLARKE

CHAPTER 4: HOW TO AVOID CODEPENDENT RELATIONSHIPS

If you recognize that engaging in codependent relationships is a pattern for you, or if your most recent relationship featured codependency, chances are you are wondering how you can avoid having a codependent relationship again in the future. Avoiding codependent relationships largely requires you to begin doing inner work and healing yourself from the effects of codependency so that you do not find yourself heading straight into another codependent relationship.

Before you can genuinely and confidently engage in a healthy relationship with others, you need to understand how you can engage in one with yourself. Knowing how to overcome the beliefs and experiences that lead to you becoming codependent in the first place is essential in helping you see yourself as valuable and worthy of experiencing positive, healthy relationships.

The following seven sections are going to detail essential steps that you need to take in order to prevent yourself from engaging in a codependent relationship once again or for the first time. By investing yourself in healing these aspects of yourself and your life, and adjusting your perception to recognize the value that you have to offer the world just as you are, you increase your chances of entering a healthy, normal relationship free of codependency.

Step One: Set Boundaries

Individuals who are codependent often struggle with inner boundaries—the boundaries that are responsible for helping them be perceptive and engage with the world as an individual who is separate of others. This is how codependents allow other people to walk all over them by taking advantage of them and exploiting their generosity and giving nature. Learning how to overcome codependency requires you to understand the importance of boundaries and how you can begin enforcing personal boundaries in your life, both in how you let others treat you, and in how you treat others.

According to LA-area therapist Darlene Lancer, LMFT, love cannot exist without boundaries, and many codependent individuals do not recognize this. As a result, they end up giving their material belongings, emotions, energy, resources, attention, and affection to anyone who might be able to fulfill their need of feeling important and purposeful in life.

The codependent struggles with boundaries, especially because they are an over-giver, do not have a clear understanding of who they are, do not feel that they have any rights, or they think setting boundaries will jeopardize the relationship or lead to rejection. In some cases, the individual was also never taught how to set healthy boundaries, therefore, they simply have no idea as to what it means or how to create them. The codependent's lack of boundaries leaves them open and vulnerable to being taken advantage of by others, which results in codependency building or being reinforced by the relationships they enter.

If you are no longer in a codependent relationship, learning how to establish boundaries is the first thing you must do. By learning how to establish boundaries, you can ensure that you are no longer leaving yourself open and vulnerable to individuals who are likely to take you for granted, take advantage of you, or leave you feeling as though your needs are going unmet. This means that you can begin learning how to engage in healthy relationships where you teach people to treat you in a healthy manner, and you are able to also treat them in a healthy manner as well.

Setting boundaries requires you to understand what your needs are, as well as what you are willing to accept into your life and how you are willing to accept it. Knowing how to set boundaries requires you to also learn how to say "no" without feeling the need to over explain yourself or experience immense guilt afterward. You can do this by practicing saying no or setting boundaries in smaller ways, such as with people you do not share a close relationship with.

In these circumstances, it feels as though there is a lot less pressure to behave in a certain way so it may feel easier for you to practice. Then, as you grow used to it, you can begin asserting your boundaries in other relationships, too. It is important that you do this before getting into any intimate relationships to avoid having yourself become vulnerable to another codependent encounter due to your lack of boundaries.

If you are feeling particularly unsafe or uncomfortable in setting boundaries, you may benefit from sitting down with a journal and genuinely reflecting on where your lack of boundaries has impacted you and how. This can give you the opportunity to understand situations where you wish you should have said no or requested that you be considered in a more respectable way.

Then, you can begin to discover what boundaries would have supported you in having those needs met and begin asserting those boundaries going forward. It may take you some time to feel comfortable with asserting them, so continue practicing and affirming your rights until it becomes easier. Regular practice will help make asserting yourself feel more manageable, which should help you in enforcing your boundaries in relationships.

Step Two: Let Go of People-Pleasing

At some point in your life, chances are that you learned that in order to continue receiving love and affection, you needed to give up on your own needs and desires in favor of someone else's. Leon F. Seltzer, PhD, mentions how people-pleasing often stems from childhood and is used as a way to please our parents so that we can receive positive attention from them.

In dysfunctional families or relationships, the amount that a person has to accomplish in order to receive positive attention may be unreasonably high and combined with being shamed or attacked for not achieving those standards. As a result, the child or person develops an obsessive need to make others happy through perfectionism and feels an immense sense of shame any time they do not feel that they have adequately met the expectations of others.

Seltzer claims that if you are a people pleaser, chances are you have a harder time saying no to people and you are more likely to let your guard down and allow them to cross over boundaries in order to please them. This leaves you extremely vulnerable to being negatively impacted by codependency in your relationships, as people like addicts or abusive individuals prefer someone who will make it easy for them to take advantage. Not releasing your people-pleasing tendencies can result in you leaving yourself open to entering a codependent relationship once again, which is something you want to avoid.

People-pleasing is a particularly challenging trait to overcome since many people-pleasers find themselves believing that if they were to stop behaving in this obsessive manner, they would not receive love, attention, or approval by others. Of course, this is not true, but the mind of a codependent people-pleaser struggles to genuinely believe that they can receive love even if they do not go to great lengths to impress others. Overcoming this trait will require you to stop giving into people-pleasing as well as learning to validate yourself and approve of yourself and your right to experiencing love and appreciation in life.

The ultimate goal when it comes to overcoming people-pleasing is for you to learn how to validate yourself so that you don't need anyone else to do it for you. This requires you to begin building a relationship with yourself and establishing positive self-esteem and self-confidence so that you stop letting people exploit you either accidentally or on purpose.

For example, say you are involved in your child's parent advisory council and for the past few years, you have taken on more than your fair share because other parents do not want to engage in the activities and you feel that you must do it to please them. In this circumstance, you need to learn how to say "no," assert your boundary, and then validate yourself and approve of your own choice so that no one else's opinion of you and your decision matters.

Seltzer says that learning how to approve of yourself and validate yourself is less about changing your actions and behavior and more about changing how you approach things in your life. According to his research and findings, learning how to recognize that you are deserving, and affirming that deservingness supports you in realizing that you can stop doing things that feel burdensome and begin doing more of what makes *you* happy.

You can also spend time rationally thinking about the situations you enter and genuinely determining whether or not you will be rejected if you choose in favor of yourself. If you will be, determine how much that rejection genuinely means to you and if you truly want to value it more than you value yourself.

Step Three: Become Responsible For Your Own Happiness

In codependent relationships, the codependent partner often struggles to generate their own feelings of happiness and finds themselves struggling to feel happy and complete without someone to depend on. If you are no longer in a codependent relationship, you may find yourself feeling uncomfortable, lonely, or even miserable because you are not sure as to how you can generate happiness for yourself.

It is likely that in your codependent relationship, you found yourself going to your partner and using them as a way to generate happiness in your life. Any time you were not with them, even if you were in an enjoyable setting, you may have found it hard to experience happiness because your partner was not there with you. This means that you are not taking responsibility for your own happiness and that you are unable to genuinely feel happy on your own without the affection and approval of the person you are codependent with.

It is important that you learn to create happiness in your own life so that you no longer find yourself trying to place your ability to feel happy with someone else. This will keep you from feeling as though you have to quickly hitch up after a breakup with the next person who is willing to enter an unhealthy relationship with you so that you can start feeling happy again.

Taking responsibility for your own happiness may not seem easy, but learning to do so is extremely liberating, especially for someone who has not been able to effectively feel happy on their own. UT Austin professor, Dr. Raj Raghunathan, did a report in 2011 that he later evolved into a TED talk on taking responsibility for your own happiness. He discussed why some people struggle to do this and how they can begin overcoming their need to have someone else in order to make them feel good.

What he found from his research was that many people genuinely believed that their environment and those in their environment all made a significant contribution to their ability to feel happiness. These people believed that if their environment or those surrounding them were unhappy, then they too must feel unhappy. As a result, many of these individuals were unhappy.

For the people who reported that they were happy in their lives, Raghunathan realized that they largely agreed that their happiness had nothing to do with their circumstances. Instead, it was derived from their own inner state and their choice to feel and experience happiness in their lives regardless of what was going on in their environment or with the people around them.

These people had effectively learned to take responsibility for their own happiness which resulted in them experiencing the sustainable happiness that was not able to be taken away from them unless they stopped choosing to be happy.

Raghunathan reported that for people who wanted to genuinely choose happiness, they first needed to build confidence in themselves and in their right and ability to choose happiness. Building confidence in yourself starts by genuinely getting to know yourself and understanding who you are, what you need, and what you want in life.

Through getting to know yourself, it becomes easier to feel confident in your understanding of what will make you happy and how you can begin engaging in your life in a way that cultivates happiness and joy. This way, you can begin genuinely creating your own happiness and not relying on others to create it for you, and you can confidently say "no" to or walk away from anything or anyone that does not support your happiness.

The next time you enter a close or intimate relationship, such as with a potential lover, it is imperative that you hold onto knowing what makes you happy and how to cultivate happiness in your own life. This will allow you to detach from the other person in a healthy manner that supports you in continuing to generate happiness whether or not they are around.

That way, you can avoid entering another relationship where you do everything to keep your partner happy, and worry that you yourself will not experience happiness if it is not being experienced with your partner.

Step Four: Be Realistic About Emotional Intimacy

In individuals who experience codependency, their ideals on what emotional intimacy entails and how it impacts a relationship can be challenging. Many codependent individuals struggle to decipher the difference between being emotionally intimate with a friend versus being emotionally intimate with a romantic partner. As a result, they may find themselves confusing their platonic relationships with ones that include romantic feelings, such as a crush.

This can lead to them struggling to establish healthy relationships, overstepping boundaries, and even finding themselves feeling as though they are betraying their romantic partners when they engage in close relationships with others. It can also lead to feelings of jealousy when their partner establishes an emotionally intimate friendship with another person, due to their confused beliefs.

As you are no longer in an active codependent relationship, it is important that you learn to begin establishing a strong understanding of emotional intimacy and how it works in both platonic and romantic relationships. This way, you can begin feeling confident in engaging in emotional relationships with people without perceiving them to be more than they are or unconsciously exploiting them to serve your emotional needs.

If you struggle to experience emotional intimacy in an effective manner, chances are that you may find yourself struggling to understand the nature of the relationships you enter and the roles of each person involved. You may find yourself expecting more from the other person than is reasonable in your relationship, or you may find yourself struggling to be vulnerable with them for fear of what it may result in.

For example, if you were abused as a child and being emotionally vulnerable was shamed, you may find yourself struggling to admit how you are truly feeling for fear of being shamed by the other person. Both a confused perception of emotional intimacy and fear of being emotionally intimate can result in you struggling to enter relationships with the ability to view them in a healthy manner.

The common consensus amongst psychologists is that codependent individuals need to learn to begin cultivating a network of friends with whom they can share genuine relationships with. This includes experiencing emotional intimacy with your friends and building genuine connections that are able to fulfill your social and emotional needs in a way that is healthy and effective—in other words: learning how to enjoy the emotional and social benefits of multiple relationships rather than attempting to gain everything you need from one dysfunctional relationship.

Learning how to be in an emotional friendship that is void of physical intimacy can be challenging if you are used to getting everything from one person. However, as you begin to cultivate more friendships and enjoy them in a healthy manner, you will discover that friendships are just as stabilizing and helpful as romantic relationships are.

The best way to begin doing this is to start building more friendships and recognizing that these friendships are strictly platonic. Then, going into the friendship, adjust your expectations to avoid getting set on the idea that this person will fulfill all of your social, emotional, psychological, and potentially physical needs for you. Instead, practice being responsible for your own happiness and learn to enjoy your friends' company as friends.

Also, practice being vulnerable and share how you truly feel and express yourself in an authentic manner without hiding behind a people-pleasing mask. This is going to help you discover how to feel fulfilled by multiple relationships without depending on any one person (other than yourself) to experience joy, connection, and intimacy.

Step Five: Embrace Time Alone

Pennsylvania based therapist Rhoda Mills Sommer suggests that codependency is more like a deep state of anxiety as opposed to something that is strictly related to addictions. In her studies, Sommer has concluded that most people who are codependent lack the ability to feel complete on their own because they were never taught how to have their needs met independently. Due to their inability to create a feeling of safety and fulfillment in solitude, Sommer claims that the best thing a codependent can do when they are recovering from codependency is learn how to spend time on their own.

Typically, codependency requires you to be unhappily entangled in someone else's agenda, fulfilling their needs, and supporting them in maintaining their lifestyle. This is commonly seen in people-pleasing and savior acts where the codependent partner does everything they can to support the other person in having their needs and desires met.

If you are the codependent person in this relationship, these behaviors lead to you not knowing or understanding your own agenda, therefore, struggling to be on your own and do things for yourself because you simply do not know what that looks like and the fear of the unknown gives you anxiety.

You may recall times in your own experiences with codependent relationships where you gave up many things in order to serve your partner and ensure that their needs were being met. Then, when they were not around, you did not know what to do with yourself because you became so used to serving your partner's needs that you did not know how to serve your own or fill your time without them. This fear of not knowing how to fulfill your needs on your own leads to intense anxiety, which creates the fear of being alone.

Sommer claims that many of her clients feel disturbed by the recognition of the reality that they no longer feel as though they can function successfully on their own. This disturbance combined with the fear and anxiety leads to codependents not wanting to spend any time alone because they are not willing to face the feelings that loneliness brings to them. In order to get past this behavior, then, you need to learn about who you are and what you want in life so that you can begin fulfilling those needs first.

This means that the best way for you to overcome the anxiety of being alone is to start spending more time alone and embracing the anxiety that arises when you do this. If you are worried about facing it on your own, you might consider involving a therapist in this equation who can chat with you throughout the process and support you in understanding the feelings that arise. This may make facing the anxiety and understanding the feelings of fear and disturbance more manageable.

In the times that you spend alone, it is important that you begin simply to avoid overwhelming yourself and causing greater feelings of fear and isolation. The best way to do this is to plan simple moments of alone time at first in an area where you feel comfortable embracing anxiety.

For example, taking yourself out on a "date" consisting of dinner and a movie at the popular plaza downtown may be too much of a leap as a starting off point. A better option would be eating dinner alone in your own home one night without calling or texting anyone or inviting anyone over.

This gives you the opportunity to begin exploring what it feels like to be alone so that you can start asking yourself important questions such as "What do I want in life?" and "What makes me happy?" It also ensures that if anxiety begins to creep in, you feel safe and secure in your space and you can surround yourself with feelings of familiarity and comfort to avoid the anxiety becoming overwhelming.

Step Six: Keep Your Life Moving

As you heal from being codependent on someone, it is important that you realize that there are still going to be many instances where codependency attempts to rear its head in your life. For example, when you meet someone new that you are interested in or that you desire to create a relationship with, your old triggers for codependency may arise once again.

This is because your healing time spent alone has been largely focused on building a stronger relationship with yourself. These opportunities are a wonderful chance for you to begin building strong and healthy relationships with others, too, to avoid succumbing to codependency once again in future relationships.

According to Erica Holtz, a licensed marriage and family therapist and co-owner of a practice in Pennsylvania, one of the most challenging parts of healing for a codependent when it comes to engaging in new relationships is not relapsing into all of the old codependent behaviors. Even though you may attract someone new and healthy into your life, you may find yourself unconsciously teaching them to treat you poorly and enter a codependent relationship with you.

For example, if they begin to naturally pull back or engage in healthy detachment, codependent tendencies might cause you to attempt to fill the void by becoming clingier and asserting yourself more into their lives. If they don't stop you, then the dynamic is perfect for codependency once again. If they do stop you, and you do not take the time to heal from that experience, it may encourage you to attempt to push yourself into another codependent relationship as soon as possible to fulfill your own needs.

As you go through the process of healing, learning how to be alone, engaging in your own acts of self-care, and living life as an independent person, it is important that you maintain this level of independence anytime you engage in new relationships. This is how you can avoid getting hooked into another codependent relationship that you have been working so hard to avoid.

Each time a new person enters your life, practice engaging in a healthy relationship with them by respecting their space, setting your boundaries, and keeping your life moving even though someone new is around. Do not skip going to the gym in favor of going to see them or blow off your loved ones to spend time with them. Likewise, do not spend time obsessing over this new relationship, setting expectations of what you will gain from it, and then obsessively trying to draw them into your life as a way to have those expectations fulfilled.

Instead, focus on keeping your healthier life moving and incorporating them into that life in whatever way feels natural for both of you. This is going to support you in engaging in new relationships in a healthy manner that allows you to continue nourishing yourself and your needs, while also enjoying the company of someone new.

If you find yourself giving up on your healthier habits in favor of this other person, or obsessively messaging them without giving them the opportunity to contribute to the relationship in their own way, it is important that you step back and address this. Take some time alone to understand why you have placed so much pressure on this relationship and what you feel that you might gain from it if you were to have it your way.

Then, allow yourself to understand why you feel as though you are not gaining that in your life on your own and look for ways to begin fulfilling those needs without the other person needing to be involved in the process. This allows you to nurture your independence and develop your new and future relationships in a healthier manner.

Step Seven: Do Not Settle For Love

An extension of the high potential for a codependent to relapse in future relationships is the tendency to settle in favor of finding a partner to engage in a codependent relationship with. When a codependent person does not take the time to understand what it is that they truly want in life and in love, it can be easy for them to find themselves willing to settle on a partner so that they can experience the love that they *think* they want and need in their life. What ends up happening, however, is that they find someone who is just as toxic and unfit as their previous partner and the cycle of codependency rises once again and takes over.

If you want to avoid engaging in any future relationships that feature codependency, it is imperative that you begin learning how to set your personal standards higher. You also need to learn how you can assert these standards to avoid settling in favor of having a relationship sooner. This requires you to both know what you want in love and to be willing to wait for the right person who can offer you this type of healthy, loving relationship.

Expanding on Erica Holtz's theories from Step 6, learning how to avoid finding yourself in a future codependent relationship requires you to be willing to stand firm in your new, healthier patterns and uphold them no matter what.

Otherwise, you may find yourself quickly engaging with new people and falling into deep relationships with them before you are able to recognize whether or not the relationship is actually a good fit for you. This will only end in you finding yourself trapped once again and struggling to regain your sense of self in the midst of a new, yet again damaging relationship.

The best way to overcome your likelihood of settling in relationships is to know in advance exactly what your standards are and to spend time asserting them in your life in general. Spend some time honestly considering what it is that you want in your life and the people in it, especially when it comes to how your relationship enriches your life and supports you.

While many would caution against having standards too low (which you should avoid), also be cautious when setting these standards to avoid setting them too high and expecting too much from people. This is a great opportunity to recognize where your existing standards may be unreasonable or failing to serve you so that you can adjust these standards accordingly.

As you get to know yourself and what you want in life and in the people in your life, you can begin embracing the process of developing new relationships. Instead of specifically "hunting" for people who fit your criteria, focus on just living your day to day life and allowing these relationships to arise naturally. As they do, spend some time engaging in the relationship and see what happens.

If the person you are engaging with does meet your criteria of what you are looking for, then you know that you can continue building a healthy relationship with this person. If they don't, you can release the relationship and move forward with your life, trusting that new people will arrive who are a better fit and who will engage in a healthy, productive relationship with you.

CHAPTER 5:
HOW TO FIX YOUR CODEPENDENT RELATIONSHIP

If you are currently in a codependent relationship, you might be wondering how you can fix this relationship to eliminate the codependency and support it in returning to a healthy, wholesome state.

Many resources claim that codependency cannot be eliminated from established relationships, but this is not true. The truth is, it will be challenging and will require great commitment, but the process of fixing your codependent relationship can be successful if you remain committed and stay determined.

As you embark on this process of mending the relationship, realize that it *does* take two to tango. In other words, there is a possibility that you could begin embracing the healing process and overcoming codependency but your partner may not be willing to accept those changes in the relationship.

If this is the case, it may be beneficial to step back or even consider ending the relationship to ensure your own health and happiness. However, if you do assert yourself effectively and you begin noticing changes in the relationship, there is always a chance that it could improve and you two can begin sharing a healthy relationship that is free of codependency.

It is also important to note that you need to be very conscious of what mindset you approach the process of repairing your codependent relationship with. If you attempt to approach it with the desire to control or "fix" the other person in your relationship, you are still approaching it with a codependent mindset. The goal here is not to fix the other person or pressure them into experiencing a healthier and more productive relationship with you.

Instead, it is to change your own actions, behaviors, and beliefs and to assert that how you will allow others to treat you has changed. Hopefully, the other partner obliges. If they do not, it is not your job to ensure that they change how they treat you. Instead, it is up to you to change how you are willing to be treated, and take the proper action necessary to ensure that you are treated accordingly. In the most extreme cases, this will mean ending that relationship.

In this chapter, we will cover seven steps that you can take to release your tendency to be codependent and create a healthier relationship. Each of these steps is imperative, so make sure that you take the time to put each one into practice to improve your relationship overall. If you are currently in a relationship, having access to a trained therapist who is educated in codependency can be extremely beneficial as this ensures that you have the adequate support to overcome your codependency and improve your life.

Step One: Stop Being an Enabling Caretaker

One of the biggest ways that codependency shows up in relationships is through the codependent obsessively taking care of their partner, thus enabling them to continue behaving in ways that are destructive to the health of the relationship and both partners. A study done at Ohio State University in 1993 discovered that only two symptoms were consistent across all psychologists' beliefs as to what codependency is and what it entails. The first symptom was excessively taking care of and taking responsibility for the other partner, and the second was being afflicted with chemically dependent individuals (which we have since learned is not the only circumstance that nurtures codependency.)

But when you excessively take care of someone and take responsibility for them, you enable them to dismiss the consequences of their own actions in favor of continually engaging in destructive behavior. In relationships that are known to cultivate and nurture codependency, like those that involve addictions or abuse, this means that the addictive or abusive behaviors continue because the individual responsible does not have to face the consequences.

In secondary relationships, or ones where the codependent latches onto a new relationship and teaches the new partner to feed into the codependent dynamic, this can result in subtle yet impactful instances of neglect and disrespect. In either circumstance, it leads to tremendous pain and suffering for the codependent and an inability to foster change or growth for the other partner.

If you want to begin healing your relationship from codependency, you need to stop trying to take care of your partner and let them begin taking care of themselves. This can feel cruel at first, even like you are engaging in tough love, but it is imperative that you take this opportunity to begin allowing them to learn how to take responsibility for themselves and take care of themselves. Instead of taking care of your partner, you need to begin learning how to take care of yourself and put your needs first.

Learning how to stop taking care of others does not mean that you no longer do nice things for the other person or nurture the relationship that you share with them. Instead, it means that you no longer allow the other person to take advantage of you and abuse your willingness to care for them by not doing anything that does not reflect an act of self-care for yourself.

For example, say the other person has a constant emotional dependence on you and requires intense emotional support, but you yourself do not feel available to offer the emotional support they require. You can say no and request that they seek their support elsewhere. This may seem harsh or scary at first, but as you begin to enforce this boundary and stand up for your own need to nurture your own emotions, it becomes a lot easier.

This goes for emotions, resources, acts of generosity, and anything else that may encompass taking care of the other individual. If it does not *genuinely* feel good for you, you need to stop doing it and allow the other person to begin learning how to take care of themselves as you do the same.

Step Two: Stop Taking Responsibility for Others

As you saw in the results of the study done at Ohio State University in 1993, caretaking often comes with taking responsibility for the other person unnecessarily. As a codependent, when you excessively take care of someone else, you also assume responsibility for this person. Even if it is done unintentionally, it happens and it can result in serious negative consequences for yourself, which never seem to stop or ease up.

This is because you are not enforcing the other person's need to take responsibility for themselves, thus allowing them to continue to act carelessly while you assume responsibility for their consequences. Since they are not learning, they continually get into trouble and rack up new consequences, and you find yourself continually taking them on yourself and putting out fires on their behalf.

This can be exhausting and extremely frustrating for you to deal with, but you may feel obligated to stay and continue taking responsibility for fear of what these consequences may cause for the other person. Furthermore, you may feel as though you will not get your needs met anywhere else so you need to keep your current situation as "calm" as possible to avoid having your needs going unmet altogether.

It is important that you recognize that other people are responsible for their own actions and that you are, under no circumstances, obligated to take responsibility for them. Even if you have been until now, easing up and letting them take responsibility for their own actions is necessary if you are ever going to let your partner learn what troubles their actions cause.

Through this understanding, they will either be motivated to make the necessary changes, or required to live with the consequences on their own. It is in no way your responsibility to endure their consequences or force them to change. These types of thoughts and behaviors are typically the very ones that lead to people entering a codependency cycle in the first place.

Allowing someone else to take responsibility for their own actions ultimately requires you to observe what their consequences are and then refuse to take responsibility for them. For example, if your partner drinks and gets into an argument with their boss and loses their job, it is not your responsibility to fix this by getting your partner's job back or finding them a new one.

It is up to your partner to find a way to fix the mess that they have made and face the consequences of their actions. If you are being impacted by their actions, such as by not having rent paid on time due to your partner losing their job, you are only responsible for finding resolve for *yourself*. Your partner is responsible for finding their own resolve and taking care of themselves. It is not your duty to save them from their own actions.

Step Three: Release Yourself from Guilt's Strong Grip

One of the biggest reasons why codependent partners struggle to let their partner face their own consequences or take care of themselves is because they experience massive feelings of guilt when it comes to asserting their own needs. If you are codependent and you are attempting to heal the codependency in your relationship with another person, you are likely going to feel immense amounts of guilt around not serving the other person anymore. You may also feel guilty that they are having such a hard time facing their consequences now that you are no longer protecting them from having to take responsibility for themselves.

It is important that you understand that just because you are letting your partner take care of themselves and take responsibility for their own lives does not mean that you are no longer able to be supportive of them. You can still show support in healthier manners, such as through empathy and compassion.

By showing this person empathy and letting them feel compassion through you but without taking advantage of you, you enable them to begin taking responsibility for themselves but not in a way that feels harsh or cold. At first, they may disagree and attempt to make you feel guilty for pulling back, but over time, both of you will grow accustomed to the changed dynamic and it will begin feeling a lot better.

When you are able to support someone in a way that feels compassionate and kind-hearted but does not take away from your own wellbeing, it is easier for you to be helpful without damaging yourself or experiencing guilt for your lack of involvement. You can begin feeling confident and positive about your contributions to the relationship in a way that allows you to begin feeling as though you are also being accounted for and considered in the dynamic.

Letting go of guilt's grip and understanding that it is not your duty to fix someone else's life takes time and patience. You will likely find that the earliest stages of letting go of caretaking and releasing responsibility for the other person are hardest and that each time you engage in this detached behavior, it feels painful and destructive.

However, as both of you grow accustomed to this changing dynamic, asserting yourself will begin to feel more positive and you will realize that by taking care of yourself first, you can fulfill your own needs and genuinely feel better, too.

Step Four: Stand Up and Speak Up For Yourself

During her time at the University of British Columbia in 2011, speaker and wellness coach, Dr. Susan Biali, wrote about the importance of speaking up for yourself and how, in many cases, individuals who are engaged in relationships where they are being taken advantage of often don't think to speak up. This likely happens because they have been manipulated into believing that their thoughts, feelings, opinions, and beliefs do not actually matter to those around them.

This type of unwillingness to speak up for yourself often stems either from your personality type or from experiencing a time in your past where speaking up was unacceptable. Instead of standing up for themselves and asserting themselves, they stay quiet either because they think no one will listen or because they simply don't know that there is another option available to them.

It is not uncommon to believe that standing up for yourself is something that comes naturally and that if you don't have a natural knack for doing it that you must be weak and incapable. However, this belief is completely untrue and often leads to people struggling to speak up and assert themselves or request their needs to be met. When you are an adult who struggles to get your needs met because you do not know how to stand up or speak up for yourself, it can be frustrating and exhausting.

You may find yourself feeling as though you are constantly trapped doing everything for everyone else because you are not able to speak up and say no. If you are in a codependent relationship, chances are that your partner has recognized this weakness in you and has been exploiting it for their own gain, such as in our previous example of having you take responsibility for their consequences.

According to Biali, overcoming your fear of speaking up starts by honestly addressing what might happen if you don't. Spending some time considering what the likely consequences are will lead you to realize that the consequences are not that bad. If they are, if your partner is repeatedly abusive and aggressive for instance, then standing up for yourself may require you to do something that also ensures your own future safety—for example, leaving and finding refuge in a safe place where your partner cannot hurt you.

When you think your actions through and stand up for yourself in a way that protects your wellbeing and promotes your ability to live a better life, you will find that, in most cases, the consequences are truly not as bad as you thought they would be. Instead, they generally support your wellbeing and enable you to begin living a better life without the feeling of being trapped in an unhealthy codependent relationship.

Step Five: Begin Building Up Your Self-Confidence

Referring back to the study completed at Ohio State University in 1993, one of the measures that the researchers considered was self-esteem and how codependents feel in terms of their sense of self-confidence. What they realized was that codependent individuals self-scored high in their feelings of low self-esteem, depression, and lack of control in their lives and relationships.

It was unclear as to whether the low self-esteem was a symptom of codependency or a factor that increased one's likelihood of finding themselves in a codependent relationship. However, it was clear that people who were actively engaged in codependent relationships lacked self-esteem to a significant degree.

In your own relationship, you may recognize that your sense of self-esteem is rather low every time you wonder about the state of your relationship and feel as though you are being taken advantage of by the other person. When you wonder why other people have better relationships than you do and then feel as though you are not deserving of having a better relationship, this can further impair your self-esteem and lead to you feel undeserving and unconfident. Overcoming these feelings requires you to begin building confidence in yourself and recognizing your inherent deservingness when it comes to having a good life and experiencing good things.

Building your confidence in yourself largely starts with you refraining from believing that you require someone else to validate you, approve of you, or accept you as you are. Instead, you need to learn that you are "the one" for you and that no one else can fulfill your needs or care for you in the same way that you can. It simply requires you to begin understanding what your needs are, learning how to fulfill them, and growing confident in your ability to do both.

The confidence comes from consistency, practice, and a willingness to learn as you go. As your self-awareness builds, your understanding of what your needs are and how they can be met in the most effective way possible (without needing anyone else to do it for you) will grow.

This will allow you to feel as though you can truly rely on yourself and trust that your needs will always be met as long as you are the one in charge of meeting them. Through this, your relationship with yourself will grow and your confidence will too.

Step Six: Practice Being Vulnerable in a Healthy Way

Vulnerability is healthy and even necessary in relationships, but not when it comes to being vulnerable in a way that incorporates and reinforces codependency. Being vulnerable to someone because you lack personal boundaries and you take on everything they say about you is not going to support you in feeling confident or complete without this other person in your life.

Instead, it will prevent you from being vulnerable with people who can engage in healthy relationships because you will push them away with a sense of desperation and neediness. As you push everyone away through this, you will find yourself in unhealthy relationships with people who rely on other people's clinginess as a way to feel important and purposeful in life. As a result, your codependency is reinforced and you will find yourself entangled in one toxic relationship after another.

Being vulnerable in a way that is productive to your relationship requires you to open up in a way that detaches from the other person. In other words, you need to know how to express yourself and bring people into your inner world without relying on them to validate that inner world or give you the approval that you feel you lack. This places an excessive emotional burden on others that quickly drives healthy individuals away and attracts individuals who depend on you to fulfill their egotistical needs, such as narcissists.

In order to overcome codependent vulnerability in a relationship, you need to be willing to open up to your partner and confess how you are feeling without relying on them to validate you. Instead, release your expectations of how they will respond and what support you want them to show. Only share what feels constructive to the relationship. Avoid oversharing or sharing things with the desire to have these feelings validated, as this is going to reinforce codependency and prevent you from feeling complete and fulfilled by yourself.

Step Seven: Stop Punishing Your Partner

It is not uncommon for codependent people to want to blame their partner for why they have become codependent and needy in a relationship, especially if they did not (or do not recall) experiencing codependency in previous relationships.

If you find yourself wanting to punish your partner for "making you this way," it is imperative that you stop and find a way to come to terms with what has happened. Punishing your partner is only going to reinforce a negative dynamic in your relationship and increase pain rather than promote healing.

In order to stop punishing your partner, you need to realize that the only person responsible for you, your feelings, and what you have allowed to happen to you is *you*. Your partner did not force you to stay, commit to a codependent dynamic, or feel any particular way in the relationship. Instead, your lack of personal boundaries and unwillingness to get help or leave the relationship are the reasons for how you are now treated.

This may be a difficult or even hurtful realization, but the fact remains: no one can force you to think, feel, or behave in any way except for you. When you realize this, it becomes easier for you to accept what has happened and search for opportunities to take responsibility for your own happiness and begin establishing healthier expectations and boundaries in your life.

A common point where codependents start to blame their partner for their feelings or experiences in relationships is when they begin to experience jealousy or start to feel as though they lack control. This can lead to a codependent partner feeling as though they have to take back control over the relationship, so they begin punishing their partner for how they feel.

When you experience these types of situations in your relationship, it is not up to you to punish your partner and make them feel bad for you being in the situation that you are in. Instead, you need to take responsibility. If you are feeling jealous, for example, consider why you are feeling jealous.

Is it because your partner is engaging in an emotionally intimate relationship with their friend? If so, it may be your own inability to comprehend that a platonic intimate relationship is a natural and healthy part of life and that both of you should be engaging in these types of friendships.

If it is because your partner has cheated on you and they are engaging in sexual relations with other people, consider that it is your problem that you have allowed your partner to treat you this way for so long. You need to take responsibility for allowing them to treat you this way while also standing up for yourself and making a change so that you can stop being hurt by them.

Learning to assert yourself and stand up for yourself in a way that expresses your thoughts, feelings, or needs without coming across as rude and punishing is important. It is not uncommon to find yourself feeling angry and even hostile towards your partner for your experiences, especially if you find yourself blaming them for why you feel the way you do.

However, punishing them for treating you the way you have allowed them to treat you, or for engaging in healthy behaviors that you do not understand is not constructive and will not help you heal your relationship. It will only build resentment and result in your codependency patterns continuing on as nothing truly changes with this type of behavior.

CHAPTER 6:
WHEN YOUR
CODEPENDENT
RELATIONSHIP ENDS

If you have recently been engaged in a codependent relationship or you are preparing to end one and you are still feeling the repercussions of your codependency, you may be wondering how you can overcome these feelings. Before you can move on to another relationship or learn how to avoid codependent dynamics in the future, you have to begin healing yourself, first. Learning how to overcome the effects of the codependent relationship and heal from what you experienced is imperative in helping you establish a healthy foundation to move forward from.

Healing yourself after codependency is largely going to require you to look back on your previous relationship(s) as a lesson for where you went wrong and how you can begin adjusting your behaviors in order to overcome codependency. It is essential that you be patient and tender with yourself during this process as bullying yourself for your experiences is only going to reinforce your low self-esteem and thus increase your codependent traits as you resume seeking external validation.

In this chapter, we will cover seven steps that you need to take in order to end your relationship effectively and heal from your recently ended relationship completely. This will support you in overcoming codependency and avoiding future codependent relationships so that you can begin engaging in healthy, productive, and mature relationships going forward.

Step One: Be Courageous In Ending Your Relationship

If you have yet to end your relationship, chances are you may be holding off because you are afraid of what is going to happen after the relationship ends. It is common to experience fear when any relationship ends, but especially if that relationship involves an unhealthy codependency that leaves you feeling particularly attached to your partner. Knowing how to confidently end the relationship and keep it ended takes courage and bravery, but it needs to be done if you are going to heal.

Not all relationships that feature codependency will need to be terminated, but some might. If you are attempting to heal your codependent relationship and your partner refuses to support you in this healing experience, the next step may be that you need to leave the relationship so that you can have the freedom and space to heal on your own. Therapist Darlene Lancer states that some of the hardest things you will face in your break up include the stages of blame, hope, low self-esteem, shame, and grief.

On one hand, you might find yourself blaming your partner for not trying harder or doing better, and feeling resentful that they did not engage in the healing process with you. Then, as you move through the stages of blame, you may find yourself bargaining with them and with yourself and your own expectations.

You may feel that you can adjust your expectations, lower your standards, or force them into changing so that the relationship works. At this point, you might begin to feel hopeful that things will change if you force them to, even though this never works and has never worked for you in the past.

Once you realize that blame and force don't work, you might begin feeling like you are the one to blame for your failed relationship, so you experience low self-esteem and shame. This can result in you feeling exceptionally low, maybe even experiencing feelings of depression, anxiety, and disappointment in yourself.

You might even feel them to such a great degree that you go back to the bargaining stage to avoid feeling so badly about yourself. When you finally realize the relationship is over, you will then move into the grieving stage and find yourself moving on alone.

If you are in a codependent relationship where abuse is not present, the process of ending the relationship in a healthy manner merely requires you to declare it over, leave the relationship and stay away. Ideally, you should cut all ties with this person at least for some time to avoid feeling persuaded to re-enter the relationship once more.

If you cannot cut ties for whatever valid reason, you can continue communicating with the person but should only do so on your terms and only when you feel as though you can reasonably handle the conversation without feeling compelled to rekindle the relationship or engage in codependent behaviors.

If the relationship was abusive, it is important that you take the necessary precautions to avoid being harmed by the abuse. Seeking a safe space to go, finding resources to protect you, and coming clean to your family, friends, and/or a therapist to build up your support network can be helpful in seeing yourself safely removed from that situation.

Step Two: Release Your Victim Mentality

As a codependent whose relationship has ended, you may find yourself feeling as though you are the victim of another experience that results in you feeling abandoned or neglected. This can be especially true and painful if you are someone who has experienced neglect or abandonment in your life, as these are often things that trigger people into becoming codependent in the first place.

It is important that you take the necessary action to address these feelings and understand that your ended relationship is not a case of you being abandoned or neglected once again. In fact, it is quite the opposite. This is a prime example of how you are now taking responsibility for yourself and helping yourself feel supported and cared for so that you no longer have to rely on other people, particularly toxic people, to do it for you.

Releasing your victim mentality largely comes from allowing yourself to process and heal the feelings that come along with your ending relationship. If your terminated relationship brings up feelings from your childhood, or even feelings that were perpetuated by the relationship, you need to allow yourself to grieve these memories as well as your ended relationship.

Allowing yourself to fully heal from the relationship and the triggers that the ended relationship brings up ensures that you are not going to continue to be held back by the same triggers that led to you staying in a toxic relationship in the first place.

In circumstances that are extreme or particularly sensitive, engaging in talk-therapy with a professional therapist can support you in understanding where your victim mentality comes from and how you can overcome it. Spending time adjusting your perspective and realizing that the terminated relationship is a positive change and not a loss or a negative reflection of who you are can be helpful in you releasing your victim mentality and moving on to a healthier perspective.

Step Three: Create Your Own Set of Dreams

Until now, you have spent all of your time and resources adhering to someone else's agenda and fulfilling their needs and desires in life. Through your actions, you have supported someone else while abandoning yourself and your own needs and desires, resulting in you stunting your own growth and holding yourself back from achieving anything. The reasons why may vary, but the outcome is the same: when you abandon your own dreams for someone else's, you stop setting goals for yourself and your personal growth and development stop.

According to therapist Roe Hunter of LifeWorks Counseling Center, the primary reason why codependents stay invested in someone else's goals and desires is that they lack the ability to recognize their own worth and the value of their desires and dreams. They have an easy time justifying the termination of their own goals and dreams in favor of receiving the love, acceptance, and approval that they need from the other person. This leads to the codependent not having any clear focus or direction in life, making it harder for them to do things for themselves since they are uncertain as to what needs to be done.

Overcoming your codependent relationship requires you to invest time in realizing that you are an individual who deserves to have your own set of goals, desires, and dreams in life. Then, you need to invest in actually developing goals and dreams for yourself so that you have something to actively work towards. For starters, a great initial goal to set would be to overcome codependency and develop a sense of independence. From there, the world is your oyster. You can create and recreate as many goals, desires, and dreams as you want as long as they are all yours and based on what you genuinely want for your life.

You will likely find that as you continue the healing journey, your idea of what you want adjusts. This is because early on, whether you mean to or not, subconsciously, your goals will likely still be heavily linked to the person that you have been codependent with. For example, if you had the expectation of having a great life with them as a stay-at-home spouse while they took care of you, you may initially find yourself dreaming of staying at home with someone else.

As you continue to grow apart from that relationship though and flourish into your own person, you may discover that you actually never wanted to stay at home but instead, you desire to go back to school or return to your previous career path or maybe even start a new career path altogether. Allow these dreams to develop alongside your healing journey, as they are a more authentic expression of who you truly are outside of codependency and outside of your previous relationship. Seemingly evolving goals are a sign that your independence is growing.

Step Four: Commit to Engaging in Self-Care

Living your entire life taking care of someone else can lead to you having no idea how to take care of yourself. After all, you have bypassed your own needs in favor of ensuring that someone else's needs were met and you have likely done it for quite some time. Learning how to take care of yourself in a meaningful way is an important part of healing from codependency and restoring your relationship with yourself.

At first, engaging in self-care may feel foreign and uncomfortable. According to the National Center for PTSD, self-care following toxic relationships can bring up emotions of humiliation, shame or guilt when you begin engaging in self-care because it was not only something you didn't do but something you felt that you *couldn't* do. It may feel like by taking care of yourself, you are robbing someone else of having their needs met, which is completely untrue, but a common feeling nonetheless. Allowing yourself to recognize these feelings but carry on with the process of learning the art of self-care is important.

Establishing a strong self-care routine that you can personalize and stay committed to is imperative. Your routine does not need to be excessive or fancy like the ones you read about online, either. Simply establishing a basic self-care routine around meeting your basic needs emotionally and physically can be extremely helpful. You can take a daily bath with aromatherapy oils, spend a few minutes each day meditating so that you can quiet your mind, or get a weekly pedicure or a weekly massage.

Creating a practical self-care routine will help you get used to bringing the idea back into your life so that you can begin experiencing the same level of care for yourself that you have been giving away. This will improve your self-esteem and self-worth by showing you that you are deserving of your attention more than anyone else is.

Step Five: Begin Learning To Communicate Effectively

Lancer emphasizes the importance of understanding the fact that communication is a learned skill and that many codependents have simply learned how to communicate ineffectively. In many cases, a codependent's idea of communication revolves largely around staying quiet and listening, while avoiding any circumstance that may require them to speak up and ask for their needs to be met. This ineffective communication pattern will follow you throughout your life if you do not take the time to educate yourself on effective communication so that you can begin expressing yourself in a more productive manner.

Although you no longer have a partner to heal your communication with, you do still have a strong need for effective communication. Effective communication is going to support you in asserting your boundaries, having your needs met, and engaging with healthy interactions outside of your ended relationship. It will also support you in ensuring that the relationships you may enter in the future are built around healthy communication so that you can avoid dishonesty or holding back parts of the truth, potentially leading to another unhealthy relationship.

When it comes to expressing yourself confidently, Lancer states that there are six C's you need to consider: congruency, courtesy, conciseness, clarity, cognizance, and claim yourself. This means that you want to make sure that you are keeping your messages clear, compassionate, accurate, and well-educated. You want to avoid the common codependent trait of holding back information or only telling the partial truth in favor of ensuring that you provide the other person all of the information required for your message to be clearly received.

In addition to adjusting the way you say things, you also need to adjust the way you communicate aside from your actual choice of words. Your gestures, eye contact, physical appearance, and facial expressions are also integral parts of communication. If you are presently suffering from low self-esteem, chances are your non-verbal body language reflects this each time you speak by expressing signs of nervousness, low confidence or even sadness. This means that as you focus on developing your ability to say what you truly mean, you also need to focus on developing your ability to hold yourself in a way that exuberates confidence and purpose.

When you are communicating, pay close attention to how you are expressing yourself physically. If you notice that in conversations you tend to hold back and you fidget a lot, you are informing the other person that you feel uncomfortable or even unsafe in the conversation. This can prevent you from having your needs met or asserting your boundaries effectively as it shows the other person that you are not fully willing to uphold them or even share them because you are too afraid to do so.

Alternatively, if the other individual is healthy and has no intention or desire to take advantage of you, they may find themselves wanting to end the conversation quickly because they feel as though they are making you uncomfortable. Holding yourself steady with a tall posture and a firm facial expression asserts that you are confident in what you are expressing. This makes you far more likely to be heard and have your needs met because people realize that you mean business.

Step Six: Stop Giving So Much of Yourself to Others

Following a codependent relationship, you may find yourself feeling compelled to give too much to others. This may also be paired with an inability to receive things from others, such as a constant tendency to say "no, thank you" when people offer you help or support.

Giving too much and not being willing to receive things from others likely stems from your long-term commitment to serving someone else excessively while never having received anything substantial yourself. These feelings need to be balanced so that you can begin giving and receiving equally in the relationships that you enjoy both now and in the future, whether they are platonic or romantic.

When you are giving to others, it is important that you stop and consider what it is that you are giving and why you are giving it. If you are giving something to someone else and it feels like a genuine act of love, such as a gift on their birthday, this is a positive experience of giving. However, if you are giving something excessive, or if you are giving because you feel like you have to in order to earn approval or attention, you need to refrain from giving anything and address this feeling within yourself.

For example, if you are offering to throw a party for someone you do not necessarily like or if you are offering excessive advice to someone to try and fix their life, you are giving too much. These come from trying to feel good about doing something for someone else so that they will like you more, or trying to feel good for being able to fix someone else's life in order to save them. In other words, they are clear examples of the archetypes of the people-pleaser and the savior.

Just because you are not giving things in a significant way anymore does not mean that you cannot give at all. It simply means that when you do give, you are giving from a genuine place and in a way that does not consume too many of your resources or take away from your wellbeing, and that you are willing to say "no" when what you are giving becomes too much.

Giving with the genuine desire of being nice and without any ulterior motives is important, as the biggest motive behind codependency is to gain validation when you struggle to validate yourself. Also, giving without depleting your own resources or feelings of deservingness or worth is important as it avoids you giving because you feel like you are obligated to or like you have to take responsibility for someone else's life.

Receiving is equally important, and equally difficult for a codependent or recovering codependent individual. If you have a hard time with this, chances are that your inability to genuinely receive things stems from a long-term experience of never having had the opportunity to receive anything or have your needs met in your recent relationship. As a result, it may feel extremely uncomfortable for you to receive things.

You may feel like you receiving something takes away from someone else or simply creates a feeling of embarrassment or shame around the receiving process. When you are receiving something, even something fairly small like a compliment, you might find yourself brushing it off or rejecting it because it feels undeserved or uncomfortable.

Not being able to receive prevents you from being able to engage in any healthy relationship, which requires the process of equal giving and taking. For this reason, you need to practice overcoming these fears and receiving the things that are given to you.

The best way to begin receiving is to practice on smaller things. Get used to accepting things like compliments or compassion with a simple "thank you" and without feeling as though you are now indebted to this person. Instead, realize that they have done it out of generosity and compassion and that you are not stealing or taking away from them. You are not required to reciprocate the giving by offering them something in return for what they have offered you.

They have offered and you have graciously accepted, and there is nothing left for you to do aside from say "thank you" and show appreciation for their offering. As it continues, learn to accept and receive larger things too, such as when someone offers to buy you dinner or take you out to do something. Receiving these generous acts of kindness from others helps you remind yourself that you are worthy and deserving, and supports you in engaging in healthy give-and-take relationships.

Step Seven: Stay in Your Own Lane

Lancer mentions in her research that when a codependent is healing from their relationship, they may find themselves "on the rebound," seeking an opportunity to find someone to help them get over their ex. In a rebound relationship for a codependent, the relationship is likely a toxic combination that is used to fulfill the feelings of validation that have now been stripped away from the relationship ending.

Lancer suggests that entering a rebound relationship is merely an opportunity to carry on codependent behaviors with another person, and not a strong solution for anyone looking to genuinely heal. If anything, the rebound relationship may be even more toxic than the initial codependent relationship since it is built around someone who lacks self-esteem (you) and someone who was looking for a person with low self-esteem (your rebound.)

Learning to stay in your own lane supports you in avoiding rebound relationships and not attaching onto anyone as a means of overcoming the pain and anxiety that you are feeling from your breakup. Instead, it offers you the opportunity to focus on your own healing and overcome the symptoms of codependency so that when you are eventually ready for a new relationship, you can enter into a healthy one that is mutually beneficial.

Staying in your own lane is about maintaining your energy boundaries and avoiding stepping over into someone else's life as a way to try and seek validation or gain approval from them. This means that in any relationship you share, you can easily detach from the relationship in a healthy way and continue fulfilling your own needs and desires without feeling an intense need to include someone else. That way, you can stay focused on yourself and your needs and promote a healthier balance in your own life.

A large part of staying in your own lane is realizing that you do not have control over anyone else. The only person you can control in your life is you, and if you take the time to understand this, you will likely realize that one person is plenty enough to control. Learning how to invest your control and attention into yourself may take time and practice, but with enough of it, you will discover that the independence you gain from self-control is incredibly liberating.

You no longer have to engage in relationships that place unnecessary burdens on you as a way to fill your time. You no longer need to feel as though you have to have control over others because you can successfully stay in your own lane and control yourself.

When it comes to learning how to stop taking control so that you can stay in your own lane, a great tool is to address everything in your life with the questions:

"How does this impact me?"

"How can I control myself in response to this?"

"How can my self-control serve me in this situation?"

These three questions will ensure that you are not trying to take control over anything that is not actually your responsibility. Then, you can ensure that you are only taking control over yourself in the situation and not trying to take control over anyone else. That way, you keep your expectations clear, reasonable, and about *yourself* and your own actions.

CONCLUSION

Congratulations on completing *Courage to Cure Codependency*.

By now, you should have a strong understanding of what codependency is, how it impacts people, how you may be exhibiting signs of it, and what you can do to begin curing your codependency so that you can healthily detach from people in your life and experience higher quality relationships. If you have made it this far, I sincerely want to congratulate you on your commitment to yourself and your willingness to change.

I hope that this book was successful in helping you understand what codependency is and how it has impacted your life until now. Through gaining information from experts and psychologists who are trained in supporting codependent individuals, I hope that you were able to feel confident in the information you received and its ability to support you in healing.

This is no easy feat, and it can take quite a significant amount of time to break codependency behaviors and begin experiencing total freedom from your dependency on others. I know that this time may feel challenging as you focus on overcoming codependency and nurturing your sense of individuality. However, trust that the more you stay devoted to your healing journey, the greater your chances of healing from codependency and moving forward in a healthy manner.

You can heal from this and you deserve to. The relationships that you stand to gain in your life following your healing will nurture you in a way that you cannot possibly comprehend from a codependent perspective. More importantly, you will experience a greater relationship with *yourself* that will nurture you in ways that you may not even realize are possible at this time.

After you have read this book, it is imperative that you continue on your path of healing so that you can fully recover from your codependent experience. Regardless of what stage you are in, whether you are seeking to avoid entering a future codependent relationship, fix your current codependent relationship, or heal from a recent codependent relationship, I hope that you found access to supportive insights in this book. As long as you continue following these steps and implementing them in your life, you can feel confident that you are going to experience freedom from codependency in your future.

In addition to following the steps outlined in this book, it is a good idea to continue educating yourself on codependency and how it may be impacting you in your life. By keeping this book available for future reference, you can easily look back and pay attention to the next relevant stages in your life in part two (i.e. healing or avoiding future codependent relationships).

The more you educate yourself on this pattern of codependency and understand where it comes from and why, the easier it will be for you to build your self-awareness around these tendencies and prevent them in the future. This also means that you can not only heal from codependency itself but also whatever experience may have lead to you being codependent in the first place, such as a childhood trauma or an abusive past relationship.

As a next step, you may find it important that you consider working with a trained therapist when it comes to overcoming codependency or the past experiences that led you to it. Having the support of someone who is educated on the impact of codependency and who can help you understand yourself and support you in healing can be extremely helpful. The right therapist can support you in growing more aware of who you are and what your needs are, in feeling confident in yourself and your abilities, and increasing your sense of self-worth and self-esteem.

Lastly, if you felt that this book added value to your life and supported you in any way, please take a moment to leave a review on Amazon.

I wish you all the best in curing your codependency, so that you can go on to experience a healthy, happy life filled with high-quality relationships, starting with the relationship with yourself.